DECK DESIGNS

CREATIVE
HOMEOWNER®

DECK DESIGNS

GREAT IDEAS FROM TOP DECK DESIGNERS

Steve Cory

CREATIVE HOMEOWNER®, Upper Saddle River, New Jersey

COPYRIGHT © 2000, 2006, 2009

CREATIVE
HOMEOWNER®

A Division of Federal Marketing Corp.
Upper Saddle River, NJ

DECK DESIGNS, THIRD EDITION

MANAGING EDITOR	Fran J. Donegan
SENIOR GRAPHIC DESIGN COORDINATOR	Glee Barre
JUNIOR EDITOR	Jennifer Calvert
PHOTO COORDINATOR	Mary Dolan
DIGITAL IMAGING SPECIALIST	Frank Dyer
INDEXER	Schroeder Indexing Services
ILLUSTRATIONS	Rebecca Anderson
COVER DESIGN	David Geer
FRONT COVER PHOTOGRAPHY	(top left) Dave Toht (top right) Steve Cory (bottom) Clemens Jellema
BACK COVER PHOTOGRAPHY	(all) Steve Cory

CREATIVE HOMEOWNER

VICE PRESIDENT AND PUBLISHER	Timothy O. Bakke
ART DIRECTOR	David Geer
MANAGING EDITOR	Fran J. Donegan
PRODUCTION COORDINATOR	Sara M. Markowitz

Current Printing (last digit)
10 9 8 7 6 5 4 3

Manufactured in the United States of America

Deck Designs, Third Edition
Library of Congress Control Number: 2008934548
ISBN-10: 1-58011-433-4
ISBN-13: 978-1-58011-433-2

CREATIVE HOMEOWNER®
A Division of Federal Marketing Corp.
24 Park Way
Upper Saddle River, NJ 07458
www.creativehomeowner.com

SAFETY

Although the methods in this book have been reviewed for safety, it is not possible to overstate the importance of using the safest methods you can. What follows are reminders—some do's and don'ts of work safety—to use along with your common sense.

- Always use caution, care, and good judgment when following the procedures described in this book.

- Always be sure that the electrical setup is safe, that no circuit is overloaded, and that all power tools and outlets are properly grounded. Do not use power tools in wet locations.

- Always read container labels on paints, solvents, and other products; provide ventilation; and observe all other warnings.

- Always read the manufacturer's instructions for using a tool, especially the warnings.

- Use hold-downs and push sticks whenever possible when working on a table saw. Avoid working short pieces if you can.

- Always remove the key from any drill chuck (portable or press) before starting the drill.

- Always pay deliberate attention to how a tool works so that you can avoid being injured.

- Always know the limitations of your tools. Do not try to force them to do what they were not designed to do.

- Always make sure that any adjustment is locked before proceeding. For example, always check the rip fence on a table saw or the bevel adjustment on a portable saw before starting to work.

- Always clamp small pieces to a bench or other work surface when using a power tool.

- Always wear the appropriate rubber gloves or work gloves when handling chemicals, moving or stacking lumber, working with concrete, or doing heavy construction.

- Always wear a disposable face mask when you create dust by sawing or sanding. Use a special filtering respirator when working with toxic substances and solvents.

- Always wear eye protection, especially when using power tools or striking metal on metal or concrete; a chip can fly off, for example, when chiseling concrete.

- Never work while wearing loose clothing, open cuffs, or jewelry; tie back long hair.

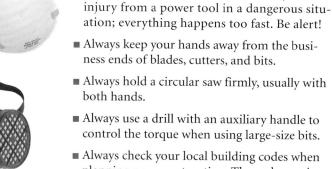

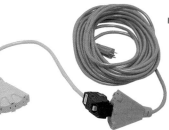

- Always be aware that there is seldom enough time for your body's reflexes to save you from injury from a power tool in a dangerous situation; everything happens too fast. Be alert!

- Always keep your hands away from the business ends of blades, cutters, and bits.

- Always hold a circular saw firmly, usually with both hands.

- Always use a drill with an auxiliary handle to control the torque when using large-size bits.

- Always check your local building codes when planning new construction. The codes are intended to protect public safety and should be observed to the letter.

- Never work with power tools when you are tired or when under the influence of alcohol or drugs.

- Never cut tiny pieces of wood or pipe using a power saw. When you need a small piece, saw it from a securely clamped longer piece.

- Never change a saw blade or a drill or router bit unless the power cord is unplugged. Do not depend on the switch being off. You might accidentally hit it.

- Never work in insufficient lighting.

- Never work with dull tools. Have them sharpened, or learn how to sharpen them yourself.

- Never use a power tool on a workpiece—large or small—that is not firmly supported.

- Never saw a workpiece that spans a large distance between horses without close support on each side of the cut; the piece can bend, closing on and jamming the blade, causing saw kickback.

- When sawing, never support a workpiece from underneath with your leg or other part of your body.

- Never carry sharp or pointed tools, such as utility knives, awls, or chisels, in your pocket. If you want to carry any of these tools, use a special-purpose tool belt that has leather pockets and holders.

CONTENTS

A well-designed and well-built deck can enrich your life—in ways both expected and unexpected. It can provide a place to get away from it all and relax under swaying branches; a platform for exciting parties or intimate gatherings; an outdoor kitchen where you can quickly whip up old favorites or experiment with new recipes; an alfresco dining room; and much more.

Unfortunately, many decks are quickly and thoughtlessly tacked on to the back of a home. Often these decks are simple rectangles, which—with luck—may provide adequate room for cooking, dining, and lounging. And they may not be too hard on the eye.

But a carefully planned deck will go beyond "adequate." You'll step naturally from inside the house to its surface, and you'll move easily from one area to the next, guided by intuitive pathways. You'll never feel cramped when cooking, dining, or relaxing, and your view of the backyard won't be obscured by railings or the deck's orientation.

A deck should look like a natural extension of the house and should provide a graceful transition to the yard. Again, planning is the key. Whether you use sophisticated design software or simply draw your plans on pieces of paper, give yourself ample time for planning both the overall look of the deck as well as the details of its construction.

Whether you plan to build a deck yourself or hire a pro, this book will

CHOOSE DECK MATERIALS that have a proven track record in your area. This good-looking deck is covered with ipé, an imported hardwood.

help you envision your future deck, so you can maximize its potential. Here you'll find a wealth of ideas, both for designing and for practical building.

THINK IN TERMS OF OUTDOOR ROOMS when planning your deck. Create spaces for cooking, eating, and a spot for just relaxing.

THE BOOK'S PLAN. The first part of this book, "Designing Your Deck," features a gallery of decks from around the country. But it's more than just a collection of pretty pictures. The photos are carefully chosen, with accompanying text that walks you through the design process. You'll learn about planning according to the way you will use

the deck, as well as ideas for choosing shapes and sizes.

The section also offers a crash course in deck building. It's not enough info to enable you to build a deck yourself, but reading it will make you an educated consumer. You'll learn how decks are built, as well as some of the major variations

due to sites and building codes.

The rest of the book features decks from four of the USA's best designer-builders. These builders use a variety of styles and building methods, suitable to various parts of the country. For each builder, you will find a profile that summarizes his design approach and building methods, as well as a gallery of some of his work.

For each builder there will be seven or eight feature decks, along with discussions of construction techniques. The drawings that accompany these feature decks give you a good idea of how they are built. *They are not complete plans, and this book does not present a complete set of how-to instructions.* However, you will find ideas and instructions on how various distinctive portions of the decks are built.

The decks in this book have been built and tested in the real world.

As you look through the pages of this book, homeowners are using and enjoying these decks. As the writer, I have visited most of these projects, and I have often heard homeowners rave about their decks.

USING THIS BOOK. This is a deck dream book rather than a manual for deck construction. It will get your creative juices flowing and provide you with plenty of specific ideas. Because good ideas are sprinkled throughout, we encourage you to browse through the entire book.

While reading, you may encounter the deck of your dreams, and it may suit your site to a tee. More likely, you will find a deck or two that has elements you like; or you may need to modify a plan to suit your house and your yard. In some cases, you may need to, say, add additional stairs or change the railing or decking. In other cases, you may choose to meld the ideas from two or three decks to form the perfect design.

Be aware that building codes vary considerably from one region to the next, so even if you have the perfect plan, you may need to change elements to meet local codes. This book will help you understand most of these issues.

Before you begin thinking about actual construction, however, settle into a comfortable chair or hammock and enjoy this book. After all, a deck is essentially a play area for adults, so a great deck should start with some dreaming.

If you plan to build a deck yourself, use this book as a companion to Creative Homeowner's *Ultimate Guide to Decks: Plan, Design, Build.* In that book, you'll find detailed step-by-step instructions for all aspects of deck-building. However, if you intend to hire a contractor to build your deck, this book can stand on its own.

DON'T FORGET TO INCLUDE EXTRAS in your deck design. Built-in planters, benches, and storage areas make your deck more functional and attractive. This tile-covered table comes in handy when friends drop over.

DESIGNING YOUR DECK

The following pages show you how to come up with a basic design for your deck, including selecting the size, shape, materials, and style for railings and amenities.

THE DESIGN PROCESS

You may choose to hire a deck designer/builder or even an architect to do the design work for you. But the more involved you get, the more satisfying the process will be. And the more input you provide, the closer you will come to getting the deck that is best for you.

You probably don't think of yourself as a "designer," especially if you have never attempted a large building project. And it probably isn't a good idea for you to try to design a house. However, a deck is usually simple in concept and relatively small, and its shape is typically dictated by the house and the yard. That means it can usually be designed by a reasonably creative person willing to put in some time and mental effort.

THE VIRTUE OF THEFT. Start by doing what all the best architects do: steal ideas. Unless your house and yard looks just like someone else's, you usually don't have to worry that your deck will look just like someone else's too.

This book is the ideal place to start. Don't hesitate to ask neighbors or even strangers about their decks—what they like and don't like, what works and doesn't work, what they would do differently if they could rebuild. Most people are happy to discuss their decks—whether bragging or complaining.

EVEN COMPLEX DESIGNS benefit when the homeowner works along with the designer to create the deck. This deck complements the house and the yard.

START THE DESIGN PROCESS by taking a lead from your house and yard. The size of the deck should be in proportion to the house, and the materials you select for decking, railings, and accessories should complement the materials used on the house.

DRAW, DISCUSS AND REDRAW.

Discuss with family members what they would like the new deck to "do." They may come up with practical ideas, such as providing shade or container gardening, or creating an easy pathway for carrying out the garbage. Or they may have definite ideas about how the deck should look. Some members might want a large deck, while others enjoy the yard so much that they would prefer a small deck.

Design software is an excellent way to "build" a deck onscreen, but it's not necessary, especially at the start of the process. Try simply making some rough freehand sketches, using graph paper to keep things to scale.

Or take a photo of the portion of your house and yard where the deck will go. (It may help to get up on a ladder, to get a somewhat aerial view.) Make several enlarged photocopies of the photo, and draw sketches of your deck onto the photocopies.

Give yourself plenty of time. Spend a few hours noodling up some initial plans; then allow a few weeks or even months for the ideas to gestate. Put your drawings on the refrigerator or the family bulletin board so you, your family, and friends can add their two cents' worth.

Don't be discouraged if some ideas are rejected or if some plans look dull on second or third consideration. The best movies leave many scenes on the cutting-room floor; you may end up with drawings in the wastebasket. That's much better than building a deck that is less than the one you wanted.

DON'T FORGET TO INCLUDE EX-TRAS, such as built-in seating and planters, top when designing. Think about how you want to spend your time on the deck.

REMOTE STRUCTURES, such as the gazebo shown to the right, can complete an outdoor living area.

A JUGGLING ACT. designing a deck involves making a number of decisions. Some will be easy—for example, you may have already settled on the decking material you will use. Others may be matters for debate—do you want a hot tub, and if so, where will it go? Here are the most common issues:

- Which of the "outdoor rooms" will you incorporate, and how will you link them with pathways?
- How can you stylistically link the deck to the house so that it doesn't look tacked on?
- What artistic or architectural element can you add to make the deck distinctive and memorable?
- How can you orient the deck so you naturally look at a scenic portion of the lawn?
- Will the deck be raised and have a railing, or can you step it down so no railing is needed?
- Which materials will you use for all of the surfaces, including decking, railings, fascia, skirting, overheads, planters, and benches?
- Will you provide for gardening, a child's play area, or any other special needs?
- Do you want a hot tub or spa?
- Where do you want lighting, and what sorts of lights do you want?
- How will you provide for privacy, shade, and perhaps protection from the wind?
- If your yard or house presents difficulties for construction—for instance, a severely sloped yard, or a situation where the deck must be raised more than 6 feet in the air—how will you overcome these difficulties?

In the end, budget may trump some of your decisions. For example, you may need to go with your second choice of materials, or you may decide on a smaller deck so you can use the materials you like best.

If money is tight, it is sometimes possible to build in phases and work on part of a project now and leave the rest for later. Just be sure that the first part will look good on its own, and that the second part will not look tacked on.

The following pages address aesthetic considerations ("Sitting Pretty," page 18) and practical matters ("Designing Outdoor Rooms," page 27). You'll find yourself going back and forth between the two, to design a deck that both looks good and works well.

TAKE THE TIME to consider the elements you want on your deck. For example, do you want an adjoining screened-in porch like the one above?

BALANCE RAILING DESIGNS, opposite top left, with building code requirements.

MATERIAL SELECTION can make or break a deck design, as shown on the redwood deck opposite top right.

INCORPORATE THE VIEW into the finished design, opposite bottom.

SITTING PRETTY

Keep the deck's setting in mind. It probably snugs up to the house and rests on top of the backyard, meaning it will affect both architecture and landscaping. You'll never get a deck to completely blend with its surroundings—it's too distinctive a structure—but you can take steps to ensure that it enhances its surroundings, rather than clashes with them.

THE VISIBLE ELEMENTS. A deck's height, as well as the elevations of the surrounding site, determine which portions of the deck are most on display. If the deck is low to the ground, the decking will likely be a visible feature. A deck that is raised a few feet above the ground will have railings, stairs, and perhaps skirting—and these vertical elements will be the most eye-catching. If the deck is raised higher than 6 feet, its underside will be at least visible and may be on prominent display.

If a deck can be seen only from the backyard, you may feel comfortable having it look very different from the house. You may think of it as a retreat, a sort of vacation spot—so it's fine if it looks woodsy even though your house has a formal appearance. Often, however, a deck is at least partly visible from the street or sidewalk. In that case, you will probably want it to appear similar to the house.

SIMPLE OR ORNATE? If your house features straightforward, clean lines, consider elements that are similarly simple, such as a railing without ornate post caps and simple balusters (or even cable and glass); decking that runs in one direction only; and solid rather than latticework skirting. Keep visible hardware to a minimum, and avoid overhead structures with criss-crossing lines.

If your house has plenty of trim and gingerbread-like details, go ahead and install railings with plenty of lines and ornate post caps, decking in interesting patterns, and lattice skirting. An elaborate overhead will probably not look out of place.

A SLOPING BUILDING SITE or the design of the house often puts the underside of the deck in full view, top left.

INCLUDE NATURAL ELEMENTS, such as trees that grow up through the deck, top right, in the design.

LOW-LEVEL DECKS, left, usually have the decking surface on full display from the yard or street.

EXISTING FEATURES, such as the pool shown opposite, place limits on the design. The posts support a second-story deck.

SIZE. A deck should not be so large as to visually overwhelm the house, nor should it look like a little porch jutting out from a long wall. In most (though certainly not all) cases, a deck looks best if it is about two-thirds as long as the house's back wall.

The square footage of a deck is not the only thing that determines how large it appears. A low-to-the-ground deck will appear less massive than a deck that is raised and has vertical elements. Light-looking railings (perhaps with cables or glass panels) make a deck less imposing. If thick beams or other framing members are visible, they will make the deck seem more massive.

Strategic plantings can fool the eye. Placing shrubs that hide corners of a deck will make the deck look smaller; trees or large shrubs up against the house can make the house look smaller.

SHAPE. If a house wall is curved or has interesting angles, it is often a good idea to mimic those lines when you build the deck. However, most houses have rear walls that are pretty straight, perhaps with a right-angle turn or two. Decks often feature curves, odd angles, and octagonal shapes. These whimsical touches may be out of keeping with the house's shape, but a little variety is often a good thing; a deck can add interest to an otherwise bland shape. However, avoid designing a deck with a lot of wacky angles if the house has a stately appearance.

The closer the deck is to eye level,

THE LARGE DECK shown left fits the scale of the yard and house because the designer chose to step down the level in the forefront of the photo.

TWO LEVELS, BUILT-IN SEATING, AND A PERGOLA add distinction to the small deck shown above. Note how the overhead is at an angle to the deck area.

SMALL CAN BE INTERESTING, as shown in the angled steps and built-in benches of the small deck shown below.

the less apparent its shape will be to passersby. So a deck that is 3 to 7 feet tall and rests on a level yard can have lots of angles and still not affect the appearance of the house all that much.

A deck's shape often has practical functions. For instance, a simple rectangular deck may make it difficult to create several "rooms" with connecting pathways, so adding a jutting-out section or two may solve the problem. They are great for additional seating or as a cooking area.

COLOR. In the past, nearly all decks were made of natural wood that was either stained or allowed to "go gray." Today, many decks are made of composite or vinyl materials, which come in a variety of solid colors that include tan, brown, gray, beige, and reddish. There are enough available colors so that you can probably complement (or even match) your house's siding color.

In addition, you can buy railings, fascia, and latticework that is white. (White decking is not popular, for obvious reasons.) One popular look combines wood-tone decking with white vertical elements.

Natural wood allows you plenty of color choices. Even a deck that has turned gray can be cleaned and stained to the color of your choice. Recently, deck stains have been introduced in red, blue, green, and other colors. Be aware, however, that you will probably need to restain yearly.

An all-wood deck can look good with all the parts stained the same color, but a composite or vinyl deck may look bland unless you use at least two colors. You can paint railings and fascias, as long as you sand and prime thoroughly first. However, painting the decking is usually not recommended; unless applied very carefully, the paint will likely chip and peel.

THEME AND VARIATION. After you've looked through this book, you may have dozens of ideas that you'd like to incorporate into your deck. However, too many design elements will lead to a confused or busy design. Limit yourself to two or three major themes, and make other elements variations on those themes.

A theme might be a shape, like an octagon or curve. You may have one or two places where the shape is presented in a large way, and other places where the shape is repeated in smaller ways. For instance, there could be a large, sweeping curve or distinctive angle in the front of the deck and several smaller curves at the corners.

Another theme may originate from the railing design or from trimwork on the house. Often elements of the railing, such as color or shape, can be partially mimicked in the trim details, the fascia, or the skirting. Or you may use trim that matches or complements the house's trim.

A SMALL BUMP-OUT, opposite top, in the deck and railing adds design interest and provides a spot from which to view the yard or relax in the sun.

NATURAL WOOD DECKS, opposite bottom left, can be stained to change the color and then sealed to protect the wood from the ravages of the weather.

PRESSURE-TREATED LUMBER, opposite bottom right, can be used over the entire deck. Or use treated lumber for the structural components and an imported hardwood for the decking.

THE TOP RAIL, above, complements the decking boards.

FOCAL POINTS. A memorable deck will probably have an eye-catching point of interest. This can be a bench, a planter filled with lovely flowers, an artistic decking pattern, a lookout onto a stunning view, a tree around which the deck wraps, a table, an outdoor kitchen counter, or other structure built with careful attention to detail.

Whatever the focal point, don't hide it; flaunt it. Plan the artsy decking pattern so people will see it after the furniture is in place; position

IF ADDING AN EYE-CATCHING MEDALLION, above, be sure to place it where everyone can see it. Designs like this are common on composite decks.

RAILINGS AND POSTS, left, provide many opportunities for creativity. The rope gives this railing system a nautical feel.

QUALITY LASTS, as in the planter at right. Choose good materials and de-mand good work-manship from those who will build your deck.

the charming planters so they frame the view of the yard as you recline in a lounge chair. There are many possibilities to consider.

CRAFTSMANSHIP AND DETAILS.

Whether you do the building yourself or hire a pro, you'll find that most of your time and money will go toward the basics: footings, structure, the decking, and railings. So it's easy to neglect some of the finishing details that can be the difference between a good and a great deck. Pay

your contractor a bit more to execute these finishing touches, or take another weekend or two to carefully install them, and you'll thank yourself for years to come.

You'll find many examples of such details throughout this book, including:

■ Use a hidden fastener system, or have wood decking screwed and plugged. This almost always looks better than having exposed screw or nailheads.

■ Add decorative post caps.

■ Use the highest-quality lumber for the railing top cap, the trim on top of planters, and other items that will get handled or sat upon.

■ Insist on tight joints in your planters, benches, railing top caps, and other woodworking elements. Take extra steps to ensure that the joints will not come apart after a year or so.

■ At least sand, and perhaps rout, exposed wood corners to prevent splinters and add a finished effect.

OUTDOOR KITCHENS

IN MANY AREAS, especially those with warm climates, people have chosen to create outdoor kitchens. You can buy components or ready-assembled counters for a kitchen that includes a granite countertop; under-counter cabinets for storage; a sink with running water; a large grill; other cooking appliances, such as infrared burners; and a refrigerator. You can even add a stereo system or TV, a wood-burning pizza oven, and an outdoor fireplace.

To protect against rain and hot sunlight, many outdoor kitchens have solid overhead roofs; others have more casual trellis-type overheads. In arid climates, you can install a misting sprayer to keep things cool and humidified.

If the counter will be made of heavy brick, block, or stone, it needs to rest on a concrete footing rather than a wood-framed deck. You could have a low-to-the-ground deck run up to the counter, or you could build on a patio instead of a deck. Another option: build a lightweight counter using metal studs and concrete backer board finished with faux stone, tile, or stucco. Such a counter will probably be light enough to rest on a deck. (Check with your building department to be sure.) Or consider purchasing a lightweight ready-to-assemble counter, complete with appliances.

DESIGNING OUTDOOR ROOMS

Most decks are attached to the house, so it makes sense to think of a deck as an extension of the home rather than a totally new space. That way, people will walk naturally out the door and onto the deck.

GETTING THE SIZES RIGHT. A deck is really a sort of house addition, containing several "rooms" with distinct functions, even though there are no walls. And there should be clear (though invisible) "hallways" and "doorways" between the rooms. Typically, a deck has these rooms:

- A cooking area, or outdoor kitchen, which should be an easy distance from the indoor kitchen. If you have a modest grill and small preparation table, an area of about 5 × 10 feet will allow room for a cook and a couple of consultants. However, nowadays many people have much more-elaborate outdoor kitchens, which call for much larger spaces.
- The "dining room" should be large enough for your table, plus at least 3 feet on all sides so you can slide chairs out. Some deck designs contain a semioctagonal or semicircular bump-out to accommodate a round table. An area 12 feet square (or 12 feet in diameter) is usually large enough for a round table that seats six.
- A single lounge chair with a small table for a drink or reading material requires at least a 5 × 8-foot space. If two lounge chairs will share a small table, you'll want at least 8 × 8 feet.
- An average spa or hot tub needs an area about 10 feet square. This allows for a good-size spa plus a seating area. If the spa cover needs to be stored, you may need more space. (Many simply fold up and down, so no storage space is needed.)

- Paths (which might run from the house to the deck, join the deck's various rooms, or run from the deck to the yard) should be about 4 feet wide. In some cases, you may need to devise special pathways—for example, around a spa, if you expect a lot of traffic, or around dining chairs, if you plan to serve formal dinners.

COOKING AND DINING. Take into consideration the table and the grill you own or that you will buy. Most people set aside a separate dining room, but if you prefer buffet dining,

you could opt for several sitting areas instead. You may want to include small tables for buffet diners.

THINK OUTSIDE THE BOX, as the designer did when he turned a deck railing into an snack counter, opposite top.

CREATE ACTIVITY ZONES, when planning outdoor kitchen and dining areas, opposite bottom.

PLAN DECK SPACE around the furniture and built-ins you want to install on the deck, above. Be sure to leave room for paths between areas.

AN OUTDOOR FIREPLACE, above, lets you enjoy the view and the crackling fire at the same time. The overhead protection shown here keeps the owners out of the weather.

PORTABLE FIRE PITS, left, are a great way to warm up without the expense of a full-size masonry fireplace. Check with the manufacturer about safety precautions when using the units.

BUILT-IN SEATING, below, adds a sophisticated design element to almost any deck. Movable furniture is more versatile, but the built-ins are always there when you need them.

FIREPLACES. A fireplace adds a warm glow that attracts family and friends and encourages low-key conversation, perhaps while casually roasting hot dogs or marshmallows. You may find it surprising to learn that many decks—both wood and composite—feature small fireplaces. These can be heavy duty built-in units that rest on concrete footings or light units that can reside on top of a deck. They typically have a mesh cover of some sort to limit flying sparks. As long as the fire is kept to a modest size, the danger is minimal.

SEATING. Built-in benches and tables can have a handcrafted look that adds distinction to a deck. If you know that people will want to sit in a certain place, a built-in bench can be a good choice. However, benches with backs often force sitters to look at the house or across the deck rather than out at the yard. Movable outdoor furniture is usually more comfortable and flexible.

CONSIDER THE VIEW FROM THE HOUSE OR THE DECK

MANY DECKS HAVE A FUNDAMENTAL DESIGN FLAW—their railings block the view of the yard from inside the house and/or from a sitting position on the deck. Railings are typically 42 inches high, so it's not surprising.

One solution is to make the railing nearly invisible. Railings made of tempered glass panels are literally see-through. Horizontal cable rail systems or rails with balusters made of thin rods barely block the view.

Another approach is to lower the deck. If the deck is 3 or more feet above the ground, this can have the added virtue of making the underside of the deck less visible. You may choose to have two or three steps leading down from the house's door. Make the first step at least 16 inches wide to prevent tripping. Or build a series of level changes, cascading down to the lawn level. (As a number of the decks in this book show, stepping down a level is also a good way to define an outdoor "room".) If the final level is lower than 2 feet above the ground, you probably will not need to build a railing. You may be able to add benches, as shown above, but check local codes to be sure.

ENTERTAINING SPACES. Think about the sorts of gatherings and parties you typically enjoy, and make sure you have the right spaces to make everyone comfortable. For intimate gatherings with a few friends, a small seating area—perhaps a semicircle around a fireplace—will do nicely.

For larger get-togethers, you probably don't want a single spacious area. Parties tend to break up into groups, and for these, medium-size nooks and platforms work best. A stairway, especially if it is extra-wide, often becomes a favorite place to sit and converse while gazing at the yard.

LIGHTING. These days, decks are almost always illuminated with low-voltage lighting, available in an appealing variety of styles and types. Local codes may require that a stairway have riser lights on every other step. Other fixtures fit into posts, are attached to vertical

BUILT-IN PLANTERS, opposite, can indulge a passion for gardening, and they can be used to separate activity areas on a deck. This planter is used as a base for a small pergola.

LIGHTING PLANS, below, can add a distinctive final touch to a deck design. Lighting should be attractive and practical. Note the safety lighting installed in the step risers on this deck.

surfaces, or can be stuck into the ground near the deck.

In most cases, low-voltage lighting can be run without too much trouble after the deck is built. Low-voltage cable is actually a thin cord that can be stapled to the underside of framing or railing members, where it is barely visible. However, if you plan the lighting ahead of time, it will be easier to run the cable through joists, posts, and other members, so it will be completely hidden.

GARDENING. People who hate planting and weeding in a ground-level garden often find that taking care of plants is a pleasure when they are in a raised planter. No need to get down and dirty on your knees, and if you have a planter/bench, you can sit comfortably as you garden.

A planter can be used in two different ways: you can actually fill the planter with soil, or you can use it as a container for potted plants. The advantage of the second option is that you can easily move plants around and replace a depleted plant with one that is coming into bloom.

Make sure a planter is made of very rot-resistant materials. The best method is to slip in a plastic or galvanized metal liner so that the wood does not get wet. (The liner may need to be custom made by a sheet-metal fabricator.) Be sure there are holes in the bottom to allow water to drain out—and make sure that the dripping water will not harm anything below.

THE PORCH OPTION

MORE AND MORE, people are choosing to have part of the deck covered with a roof and encased in screening. Once you do that, you have a "porch" rather than a "deck." A porch does not have the open feel of a deck, but it has definite advantages. You can use it comfortably during a rainstorm or a buggy summer evening, and you can install electrical receptacles, an overhead fan/light, and electrical appliances.

One popular configuration is to place the porch section just outside the kitchen door so that you pass through it on your way to the deck. That way, you have a more gradual transition to the out of doors, and you don't have to get wet in order to reach the porch on a rainy day.

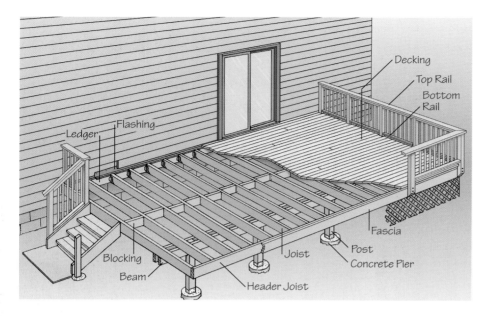

Decking
Top Rail
Bottom Rail
Flashing
Ledger
Fascia
Post
Concrete Pier
Joist
Blocking
Beam
Header Joist

basics of deck building so that you can be an informed customer.

UNDERSTANDING THE PARTS

The illustration at left shows the basic elements of a typical deck. Not all decks will have all these parts, but your deck will have most of them. We'll start at the bottom and work up.

A **pier**, also called a **footing**, is a solid piece of concrete that supports the structural **posts**. The size and shape of the footings, as well as whether they rise above the ground or not, is determined by local codes. If the footing rises above grade, there is a post anchor, a metal connector that keeps the post from moving and holds the post a bit above the

PUTTING IT TOGETHER

The basic deck is a pretty simple structure, although some deck designs can be quite elaborate. The following will not tell you all you need to know in order to build a deck, but it will acquaint you with the

concrete so it can dry out. Structural posts, usually made of 4x4 or 6x6 treated lumber, are vertical members that support the deck. A **girder**, also called a "beam," is made of massive four-by lumber or two or three two-bys laminated together.

The girder supports the **joists**, regularly spaced two-by pieces that support the decking. Sometimes short pieces of **bridging**, or **blocking**, made of the same material as the joists, are attached as shown along the middle of the joist run to provide extra strength and stability. At the house, the joists usually tie to a **ledger**, which attaches to the house. If the house's siding is cut out to accommodate the ledger; **flashing** is used to waterproof the joint. In the case of a freestanding deck, there is a girder (with footings and posts) near the house and no ledger. Outside joists and the **header joist** form the outside frame of the structure. **Fascia** boards sometimes dress up the outside joists and header. **Decking boards** sit on top of the joists, fastened with screws, nails, or special hidden fasteners. Wood decking is usually made of ⁵⁄₄x6 or 2x6 lumber. Composite decking is typically 1 inch thick and 6 inches wide.

The most common railing arrangement, shown here, employs a horizontal **top and bottom rail**, to which are attached vertical 2x2 or 1x4 balusters (also called "pickets") evenly spaced between the railing posts. A rail cap tops the whole thing off.

Stairs are made with stringers, the downward-angled 2x12s on the sides, which supply the support. The width of the stairs will determine the number of stringers necessary. Check local codes for stringer requirements. Treads are the steps you walk on. A tread is commonly made of a single 2x12 or a pair of 2x6s. Risers, usually pieces of 1x8, often cover the vertical spaces between the treads.

EXPOSED DECK FRAMING is shown opposite. Note the different directions of the joists on the upper and lower levels. That means the decking will be installed in different directions as well.

DOUBLING TWO-BYS, right, is a common way to create support beams for decks.

RAILING SYSTEMS, below, consist of support posts, top and bottom rails, and evenly spaced balusters. In this system, sleeves slip over pressure-treated posts.

ATTACHING THE LEDGER, right, is an important part of construction. It must support the deck while keeping water out of the house.

POSTS SUPPORT BEAMS, below, that hold up the deck. Notching the post is one method of supporting the beam.

FLASHING STOPS WATER, opposite. The copper shown is the second of a two-step process.

THE LEDGER ATTACHMENT. If your deck will attach to the house via the ledger, pay close attention to how this will be done. The attachment must be strong, and it must be watertight to prevent water from entering your house and damaging it. There is a variety of opinion on ledgers, and this book shows several options. In the end, local codes may determine how you will construct it.

Some prefer to cut out the siding so that the ledger attaches to the house's sheathing. If this is done, be sure that there is flashing—usually, two pieces are better than one—that prevents water from seeping into the house. Others use a hold-off method, which separates the ledger from the siding so that the area can dry out between rains.

Often lag screws secure the ledger, but some more severe codes require that bolts run through the house's framing and into the basement or crawl space. For the greatest strength, special ledger hardware is used.

PROTECTING YOUR DECK

Unfortunately, it is not unusual for a deck to start rotting within a few years, or for exposed boards to become weathered and cracked. Be sure to take steps to ensure against this.

The builders in this book are very much concerned about building decks that will look good and stay strong for decades. They come from various parts of the country, and they choose materials and techniques that will be the most durable in their climates. If for example, you live in a moist clime, be sure to check out Kim Katwijk's methods, which have been refined after years of building in the Northwest. (See page 134.) If your area is dry and the sun will beat down on your deck mercilessly, Shawn Miller of Colorado will no doubt have some ideas for you. (See page 182.)

PLAN TO HIDE THE UNDERSTRUCTURE

FOOTINGS, POSTS, AND BEAMS do their job admirably well, but are often less than pleasant to look at. You may choose to hide the underside of your deck by installing skirting. If the deck is not too high, however, it is often simplest to have the joists and decking overhang—or cantilever—several feet out from the beam. This will make the footing, post, and beam less visible from at least one point of view.

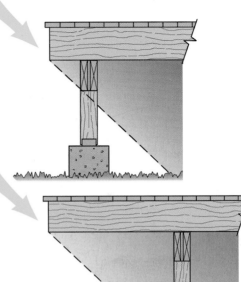

PART ONE: DESIGNING YOUR DECK

THE LABEL ON PRESSURE-TREATED LUMBER contains important information, including the type of preservative used—it is on the back of this label.

LUMBER THAT HAS BEEN TREATED CORRECTLY will show signs of the preservative material sinking deep into the wood. Be sure to use the correct lumber for the application.

DECKING MATERIALS

The materials you choose go a long way toward determining the quality and the appearance of a deck. A large number of manufacturers are competing for your business, so you have a good variety of options.

STRUCTURAL MATERIALS.

Pressure-treated lumber is the universal choice for a deck's structure. Be aware, however, that there is a good deal of variety among treated boards. For instance, in roughly the eastern half of the country, Southern yellow pine is the most common species used. It is strong and stable, and it accepts the treatment readily. In roughly the western half of the country, Southern yellow pine is not available, and "hem-fir" lumber is used instead. Hem-fir is a general designation that includes five or more species of hemlock and fir. These boards are often not as stable or strong as pine and may not accept the treatment as well. Douglas fir is perhaps the most strong and stable wood and is available throughout much of the country, but it usually has a pattern of incisions made

during the treating process, and these incisions won't disappear over time.

Older treated lumber was infused with CCA preservative, which contains arsenate and has been banned for most residential use. Newer treatments, whose treatments have names like alkaline copper quaternary (ACQ) and copper azole (CA), are safer. The label on a treated board gives plenty of information, but the general rating is the most important datum. If it says "above grade," it should be used only where it will not stay wet for prolonged periods. Use

"ground contact" lumber for boards that will come within several inches of soil or that will remain wet for days at a time.

A board's grading is also important. In general, use boards that are rated "No. 2" or better. Lower grades may warp or have structural defects such as cracks and decay. "Select" or "No. 1" lumber is even better, and should be used where the boards will be visible. Boards rated KDAT (kiln-dried after treatment) or S-Dry are low in moisture content, making them unlikely to warp or shrink.

UP TO CODE

WHETHER BUILDING YOURSELF OR HIRING A PRO, you will probably have to make sure your new deck meets local building codes. You will need to satisfy an inspector, who will likely pay special attention to the footings, the ledger, joist sizing and spacing, the stairway, and the railing. Be sure to get your plans approved before you begin, and post a permit. You will probably need to schedule and pass two or three inspections.

COMPOSITE MATERIALS, as well as redwood and cedar, make for attractive decking surfaces, but the support structure of most decks usually consists of pressure-treated lumber.

SYNTHETIC MATERIALS, left, are gaining in popularity. Most products include a proprietary attachment system.

IMPORTED HARDWOOD, such as ipé shown above, are becoming popular in many parts of the country. The wood is beautiful and durable, although the wood is so hard that installation requires special techniques.

SYNTHETIC DECKING. Synthetic decking and railing materials have blossomed in popularity of late. They promise very long life and low maintenance—and some deliver on those promises better than others. There are basically two types: composite, which combines recycled plastic and waste wood products, and vinyl, which has no wood and usually uses virgin, rather than recycled, plastic.

People like synthetics because they are low maintenance. Synthetics do need to be kept clean, however, or at least in some climates they will develop mold or mildew.

Some synthetics perform better than others. Lesser-quality products fade in color, are easily scratched, are subject to staining, attract mildew and mold, and will swell when they get wet. High-quality products resist most, if not all, of these problems. So ask builders and inspectors which manufacturers they recommend for your area. The harder the board's surface, the better. Find out what the boards are made of. In general, polyethylene is soft; standard polypropylene is harder; and high-density polypropylene is the hardest and most durable.

IRONWOOD. Also called Brazilian or tropical hardwood, species like cambara, pau lopé, and ipé are very strong, virtually free of knots, and will remain rot-free for decades. Ironwood is often similar in price to synthetics, but it may cost more to install because it is so hard. You can just let ironwood weather to a silvery gray color, but you must clean it regularly. Most people choose to stain and seal it yearly.

REDWOOD. Redwood is available only in limited locales, where it remains popular. It is soft but stable and beautiful. Choose a grade that is all or mostly composed of the dark "heart" of the wood; the light-colored sapwood will rot quickly. You can restain redwood yearly or allow it go gray.

CEDAR. Now a fairly inexpensive option, cedar is most often available

REDWOOD DECKS, right, continue to be popular in many parts of the country. With proper care, a redwood deck will last for years.

CONTRASTING BORDERS AND MEDALLIONS, right, are common design features of composite decks. However, design features like these require special blocking for attachment.

as ⁵⁄₄ decking, which is 1 inch thick and has rounded edges. Be aware, however, that today's cedar is mostly made of light-colored sapwood, which will rot quickly if not sealed. If possible, stain and seal cedar before installing it so that the undersides of the decking will be protected.

TREATED DECKING. Pressure-treated pine is often the least expensive option, but receding in popularity in favor of synthetics and ironwood. Be aware, however, that if you use good-quality treated wood (preferably Southern yellow pine in the eastern part of the country), it can be stained and will last a long time.

PART TWO

MEET THE DESIGNERS

For this, the second edition of our Deck Designs book, we chose four of the country's best deck builders, representing four regions: John Lea hails from Atlanta, Georgia; Clemens Jellema builds in Baltimore and Washington, D. C; Kim Katwijk works in Olympia, Washington; and Shawn Miller represents the Denver, Colorado area. Each has a distinctive style, suited to the region in which they live—though they all would work well in any part of the country.

JOHN LEA of DeckSouth builds in the Atlanta area. Examples of his work appear on this page.

CLEMENS JELLEMA builds in the Washington, DC, area. Some of his work appears on this page.

All of these designers have experience actually constructing decks. Some still strap on their tool belts and build from time to time, while others spend all their time designing, working with customers, and supervising work crews.

In choosing decks to include in this book, we first looked at the builder's photographs, usually found on their Web sites. Then we visited the decks ourselves and took our own pictures—both of the overall designs and of the details that make each deck special.

KIM KATWIJK builds in the Northwest. Some of his work appears on this page.

In some cases, we were looking at newly built decks, but many of the decks featured in this book are from 2 to 7 years old. We selected older decks so that you get a glimpse of how your deck could appear in years to come, as long as it is built well and maintained regularly.

For each of the four builders you will first find a section discussing his design approaches and a gallery showing off his work. The next section identifies the builder's signature building techniques—which often go above and beyond code requirements to achieve truly superior decks.

Then you'll find, for each of the builders, more detailed treatments of eight or so specific decks. Drawings and photos show how to construct the deck's framing, decking, railing, and special features. Whether you build a deck yourself or hire a pro, you can glean a wealth of information from these decks to help you plan and achieve your dream deck. The designer-builders are happy to hear from you via email or a phone call should you want to purchase a complete plan or—if you live in their area—hire them to build a deck.

SHAWN MILLER builds in the Denver area. Some of his work appears on this page.

MEET THE DESIGNERS

DECK-SOUTH

John Lea
Decksouth
Marietta, Georgia
(770) 452-3325
www.decksouth.com

DECKSOUTH

As the name of his company indicates, John Lea of DeckSouth in Atlanta, Georgia, builds decks suited to the southern temperament and the southern climate. Life in these areas moves a bit more gracefully, and people often take the time to entertain formally outdoors. As a result, many of his decks tend to be classic and stately rather than rustic and informal.

Lea finds that the design process is usually collaborative. If there are two clients involved, each will usually have their own ideas, but in the end neither "wins" over the other; Lea finds ways to make both happy. One may want a spacious grilling area, while the other may expect ample room for dinner parties and a cozy nook for more intimate gatherings. Of course, the shape and slope of the yard often dictates the shape and size of the deck. It is not unusual for Lea

to change a design midconstruction; customers may get new ideas once they see the deck starting to take shape.

THE LOCAL CLIMATE dictates the need for shade on many of Decksouth's projects. This pergola, above, provides some relief.

SECOND-LEVEL DECKS are common among Lea's clients. The arrangement usually allows for a covered patio below, right.

TROPICAL HARDWOODS

LEA OFFERS AN UNUSUALLY WIDE VARIETY of hardwoods and prides himself in knowing the characteristics of each. One of the most common is ipé, also known as Brazilian walnut. Other varieties include cambara (also known as Brazilian mahogany); garapa (Brazilian ash); and cumaru (Brazilian teak). Terms like "walnut" and "mahogany" here refer only to what the woods look like—the Brazilian versions are not related to those species. When choosing an unusual wood, Lea says, be sure it has a proven track record in your area. Ask to see a deck built of the same material that is at least 3 years old.

MOST CUSTOMERS think of their decks as extensions of the interior of their homes. The deck area is usually divided into separate living spaces, right.

EXOTIC HARDWOODS are popular choices among Decksouth's customers because of the distinctive look they impart to the deck, below.

COMPOSITE MATERIALS are popular in the Atlanta area. The railing and support posts shown opposite bottom are wrapped in vinyl.

CRISP AND CLEAN SURFACES

Because the weather is warm most of the year, Atlanta decks are typically seen as extensions of the home, rather than as completely separate outdoor spaces. It is not unusual for a customer to think of a deck as having a kitchen, dining room, and a living room.

Deck and railing surfaces are often built and maintained so they feel almost like interior floors and trim. Decksouth's customers tend to prefer Brazilian hardwoods, also called ironwoods. (About 70 percent of his decks are hardwood, and most of the others are composite or vinyl; only a few decks have treated surfaces.) Hardwood decks usually require a comprehensive maintenance program. Most people maintain their decks carefully, cleaning at least once a year and applying sealer yearly. Few Atlantans prefer to let the wood go gray. This regular maintenance is somewhat expensive, but a well-sealed hardwood surface is nearly as clean and finished-looking as an interior hardwood floor.

THE UP AND THE DOWN

In the hilly land around Atlanta, it often happens that a yard slopes downward from the front of the house to the back. As a result, the backyard is at basement level and the kitchen is one floor above. However, what most Atlantans call a "basement" is not a dark, unfinished storage space; it is usually fully functional living space, with full-size windows.

The design solution is often an upstairs/downstairs arrangement—a raised deck above and a patio or a low deck below. To get down from the upper deck without taking up much yard space, Lea sometimes installs a circular stairway. The upper deck must be built so rainwater flows under the decking and out a gutter, keeping the area below dry.

It may come as a surprise that Lea's decks often do not have overhead shade structures. Often this is because the upstairs deck provides full shade for the patio or deck below.

ADVANTAGES OF A BIG COMPANY

DeckSouth is a large company; usually, seven crews are working at once. Because so many of his customers want a patio as well as a deck, DeckSouth is geared to build both. Many people want part of the area enclosed, so Lea often builds enclosed porches as well.

Because he deals in large volume, Lea can buy lumber directly from the mills and maintains a large inventory of boards inside a sheltered warehouse. This protects boards by minimizing warping and other defects.

Lea prides himself on being a full-service deck supplier, which means that he maintains the decks for many years after building them. He keeps one crew working nearly year-round cleaning and finishing decks. He even has his own line of stain, specially formulated to last a

MOSQUITO ABATEMENT

BUGS CAN GET FIERCE in Atlanta, so people sometimes retreat into a screened porch. However, a mosquito misting system is surprisingly effective at keeping flying critters away, making it possible to enjoy an open deck even during a summer evening. A typical system, which may run to $2,500, has a network of small hoses running underground all around the deck or patio. At strategic locations, a hose emerges and travels up a tree or post and is capped with an inconspicuous spray nozzle. The system automatically sprays the area with a repellent that is extracted from marigolds and other natural insect deterrents.

full year in the heat and humidity of Georgia summers. The cleaning business is not a great money-maker, but it does lead to loyal repeat customers. It also helps Lea to keep on top of the industry by allowing him to keep tabs on how well various decking materials perform over the years.

A TYPICAL DECKSOUTH DESIGN calls for a double-decker arrangement as shown opposite. The top surface provides shade for the lower portion.

HILLY TERRAIN requires innovative design solutions. Because the underside of this deck, above, is visible from the yard, it needs to be as attractive as possible.

A SPIRAL STAIRCASE, below, solves the problem of getting from the upper to lower areas without going inside, and the stairs take up very little space in the yard.

LEA'S TECHNIQUES

■ Codes regarding ledger construction are especially strict in Atlanta. A ledger must be bolted through—not just screwed into—the house's rim joist. Often this means a channel must be cut in the drywall inside the house so that carriage bolts can be driven through the rim joist and the ledger.

■ Lea usually uses in-ground footings and posts, meaning that he digs a fairly deep hole, pours 12 inches of concrete in the bottom, and rests the post on top of the concrete so that part of the post is underground. He sometimes encounters soil that has been dug up and re-filled—meaning it is "disturbed"—to a depth of 6 feet or more. In those cases, he may need to call in an engineer to plan a footing that will not sink. He may need to dig a footing hole as deep as 12 feet, or he may use a special helical footing, which is literally screwed into the ground.

DECK GUTTER SYSTEM

■ For the structure, Lea usually uses the highest quality pressure-treated Southern Yellow pine: No. 1 grade, and rated for ground contact—even when No. 2 grade aboveground rated would pass code. He buys lumber directly from mills and stores it himself to ensure the boards will stay straight and that his decks will be free of unattractive waves and other problems.

■ To create a stately appearance on railing posts and other large visible elements, Lea often wraps them with PVC trim boards (often referred to by the brand name Azek). He used to use primed wood trim boards, but found that they tended to crack over time. PVC trim does not warp, crack, or shrink. Most types can be painted.

■ To build a spiral stairway, Lea builds the upper deck first; then has a local fabricator make a spiral stairway out of either aluminum or powder-coated iron. The cost is typically about $3,000.

■ Where a beam needs to run across a long span, Lea often purchases a glue-laminated beam, which is a product manufactured by gluing strands of lumber together. Because they are not treated for outdoor use, Lea wraps (or "clads") them with PVC trim boards, hardwood, or cedar.

PVC WRAPPED POST

SPIRAL STAIRCASE

BISCUIT JOINERY

- Where an upstairs deck covers a patio below, it must be made water-tight so the patio does not get wet. Decksouth's system uses a roofing material called EPDM, to carry water away from the house and out to a gutter.

- Where the cap rail—the top piece on a railing—is miter-cut at a corner, Lea creates a very tight joint by using a biscuit joiner to make the joint extra-tight.

- Manufactured lattice panels look fine, but Lea often custom designs and makes his own lattice, which looks great.

- Where some deck builders leave a gap between the house and the deck-ing, Lea takes special care to create a tight, neat-looking seal where the decking meets the house. (In Atlanta he does not have to worry about moisture freezing in the joint, and he uses treated lumber that he

CUSTOM LATTICE

trusts to stay rot-free.) If the house is stucco, he may actually cut away the stucco and slip the decking under-neath. On a brick home, he often covers the joint with a piece of trim.

OPEN TO THE WORLD

THIS DECK'S NON-SYMMETRICAL SHAPE GREW OUT OF PRACTICAL CONCERNS. THE RESULT IS NOT EXACTLY THE DECK THE OWNERS ORIGINALLY WANTED—BUT IT IS A PERFECT DECK FOR ITS LOCATION.

THE DECKING AND RAIL CAPS are made of cumaru (Brazilian teak), right, which at the time of building was less expensive than ipé.

DESIGN CONSIDERATIONS

The house sits on a large lot that is open to the neighbors. The owners didn't consider privacy a concern; they wanted a deck that flowed easily onto the spacious yard and that encouraged a spirit of openness. So they vetoed the idea of a narrow stairway off to the side; instead, they chose a set of stairs in the middle of the deck that starts wide and gets even wider as it travels down to a casual patio surface.

As so often happens, this well-thought-out deck replaces a smaller, rectangular deck that was slapped on when the house was built. The deck runs along about 80 percent of the house's rear wall, even more if you take the octagonal nook into account.

The basic idea of the deck is two dining/entertaining areas, with a space in the middle that leads to the yard. At the start of the design process, the owners wanted the two areas to be balanced and the same size, in keeping with the home's orderly interior. However, it soon became apparent that a symmetrical deck would not answer more important considerations.

For one thing, they wanted unobstructed views from inside the house through the set of three windows near the door. Also, they wanted an unobstructed path from the kitchen door to the yard. The door and the windows are off center from the house, so the dining area on one side needed to be smaller than the area on the other side.

They did not need a large outdoor cooking area; a small area for a grill would do. The area next to the house, just behind the larger dining area, supplied ample room.

A unique storage chest situated in front of the deck adjacent to the lawn holds bats, balls, and other sports equipment and establishes a nice connection between the deck and the yard. Also, it keeps all that stuff organized while keeping it out of the house.

CONSTRUCTION TECHNIQUES

Lea uses high-quality pressure-treated No.1 southern yellow pine for all framing members, so he has no worries about rot. If your framing material is not as good or if you live in a wet area, see some of Kim Katwijk's techniques on pages 134–181.

THE LEDGER AND FRAMING. As with most decks, framing starts with a ledger attached to the house. In the Atlanta area, ledger requirements are very strict: the ledger must be bolted to the house's framing rather than screwed to it. If you are required to bolt, follow these procedures. Cut the house's siding to accommodate the ledger; attach the ledger temporarily with screws; and install flashing as required in your area.

If the house's rim joist is exposed inside the house (say, in an unfinished basement, or if you have a dropped ceiling and can simply remove the panel), attaching a bolt will not be difficult. If, however, the ceiling is drywalled, you will need to cut a 16-inch-wide channel in the drywall so that you can reach the bolts to add the nuts and washers.

PLAN VIEW

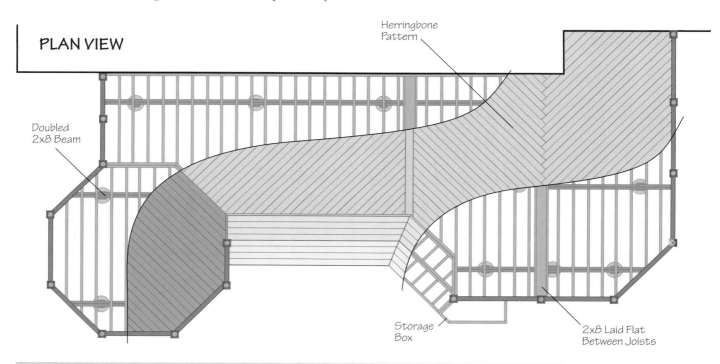

Herringbone Pattern

Doubled 2x8 Beam

Storage Box

2x8 Laid Flat Between Joists

MATERIALS USED FOR THIS DECK

Framing (all treated)	4x4 posts 2x8 ledger and joists Doubled 2x8 beams	Benches	2x4 and 2x12 cedar framing ⁵⁄₄x6 cumaru decking
Decking	⁵⁄₄x6 cumaru	Planters	Treated 2x4 framing Pressure-treated plywood ⁵⁄₄x6 cumaru for all visible pieces EPDM roofing for liner
Skirting	Cedar custom-ripped for lath 1x6 cedar		
Railing	4x4 cedar posts 2x4 cedar rails Metal balusters with plastic brackets Decorative post caps		

WHEN THE DECKING WAS INSTALLED, it was not parallel with the stair framing, left. This presented an opportunity to add an interesting detail in the form of long angle-cut decking pieces. Because Cumaru is so stable and resistant to rot, Lea sometimes attaches facing pieces and stair risers flush with the top of the deck surface, rather than overhanging the decking and tucking the risers underneath. This makes for a furniture-like appearance. But do not use this configuration if you are unsure of your materials.

DECKSOUTH CREATES RAILINGS IN SECTIONS, below, by screwing baluster-holding brackets into the top and bottom rail. The company then attaches the metal baluster to the brackets. The entire section is then screwed to the posts.

Framing the Steps

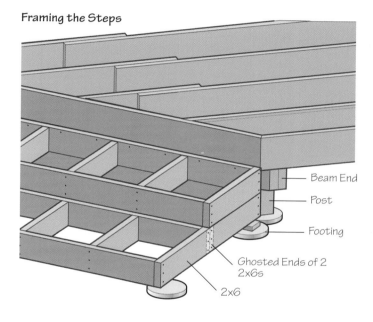

Beam End
Post
Footing
Ghosted Ends of 2 2x6s
2x6

Drill long holes through the ledger and through the house's rim joist, and tap long carriage bolts from the outside so that they protrude into the house. Codes determine how many bolts you need—often, one in every 16-inch bay between joists, and two at the ends. Add a washer; screw on a nut; and tighten. If you had to cut a channel, you will now need to replace the drywall, tape, sand, and paint—a time-consuming job.

Framing is standard. Dig postholes as required. Temporarily support the framing structure as you build. Use joist hangers at the ledger. Lea places an extra beam near the house, but many codes do not require this because the ledger can take the

place of a beam. Dig postholes as required, and install the posts. On a low deck like this, you may choose to install the footings and posts early in the process because there is not much room to work once the framing and decking are installed.

THE STAIRS. To build two wide stairs, it is usually easiest to build two framing boxes, rather than using stringers. Lea often sets the bottom frame in gravel, but you may be required to install concrete footings as shown in the drawing above.

THE RAILING. This railing uses special hardware that makes it easy to install. Attach the posts. (Lea notches

the posts on a low deck, but your codes may not allow notching.) Cut 2x4 top and bottom rails to fit between the posts. Lay out for evenly spaced balusters, and attach the baluster brackets by simply screwing them in. Slide the metal balusters over the brackets to create a balustrade section, and attach the balustrade to the posts with angle-driven screws.

On a deck with octagonal shapes you will have plenty of 22½-degree angles to cut. Take your time cutting all the large and little pieces to fit tightly; you will be looking at the railing for years to come.

For the planter, opposite bottom, start by making two simple triangular 2×4 pressure-treated frames for the bottom and the top. Cover the sides of the frames with pressure-treated plywood. Use 2×4s and another piece of plywood to provide a bottom, and drill a series of ½-inch holes in the plywood for drainage. For added protection, staple EPDM roll roofing to the insides to keep moisture away from the wood. Cut and attach decking pieces for the visible sides, the top cap, and the trim.

THE STORAGE UNIT. The owner's kids call this "the coffin" because of its shape. It is constructed like the planters, but without the EPDM liner. The tricky part is the lid. Because cumaru is so heavy, the lid was dangerous and difficult to use. The solution: Lea added a hydraulic door closer like that used on heavy storm doors. The opener is adjustable, so the lid is easy to open and closes slowly.

BENCHES AND PLANTERS. Once the decking and railing are installed, the benches and planters are custom built to fit. Start by building a 2×4 frame to support the top pieces that make up the seat of the bench. Then build supports made of 2×12 posts and 2×4 brackets at top and bottom to fit into the frame. For most people, a 17-inch-high bench is most comfortable. Cut decking pieces to fit flush to the sides of the frame; you may choose to install them a bit long, and then make a chalk line cut for perfect lines. Add trim pieces on the sides to cover the ends of the decking pieces. Lea's building crews used a router to add detail to the side pieces.

THE BENCH, opposite top, was added after the decking was installed. This bench is 17 in. high, a comfortable height for most people.

THE PLANTER, opposite bottom, features a simple 2x4 frame of pressure-treated lumber covered with short sections of decking. Lea installed an EPDM membrane on the inside.

CALLED "THE COFFIN" by the kids in the family, this storage unit holds a variety of sports equipment, right. For safety, Lea installed a hydraulic device to keep the door from slamming shut.

CUSTOM-MADE SKIRTING, made of cedar two-by lumber rip-cut to about ⅜-in. thickness, adds a handsome touch and allows air to circulate under the deck, below right. As is the case with the railing, the cedar is stained to nearly match the cumaru decking.

Custom Planter

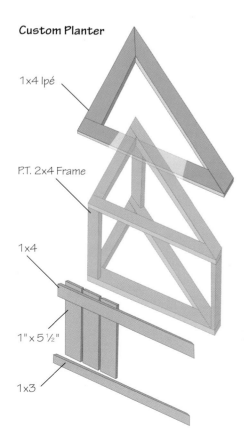

1x4 Ipé

P.T. 2x4 Frame

1x4

1" x 5 ½"

1x3

SECOND-STORY DECK
WITH
GENTLY BOWED FRONT

THIS IS A FAIRLY SIMPLE DESIGN FOR AN UPPER-LEVEL DECK WITH A
PATIO BELOW. THE CURVED "PROW" IN FRONT LENDS STYLE AND
MAKES IT A BIT MORE PLEASANT TO GAZE AT THE YARD.

BECAUSE THE DECK, above, sits above yard level, the underside framing is exposed, which is typical for an Atlanta-area design. Lea takes pains to make it as attractive as possible. As is often the case, the upper level shades a small patio below.

ROOM WITH A VIEW is one way to describe this outdoor living area, below. The gentle curve at the front end adds a bit of styling that you can't get from a straight edge.

DESIGN CONSIDERATIONS

The existing deck was small, rectangular, and painted—a recipe for homeliness. The joists and the beam were no uglier than usual, but because the deck is raised, they were on display. In fact, the framing is one of the deck's most visible elements when viewed from the yard. So the new deck needed to look good from all sides.

A SIMPLE BUT ELEGANT SHAPE. The owners weren't looking for a cooking center or a dining area, just a fairly spacious living room. Because the deck would have only one function, there was no need—as with most decks—to think in terms of separate "rooms" and paths between them. The house has a 7-foot-deep, built-in, raised patio just behind, so a deck with an area about 14 feet square would do nicely.

Though their needs were simple, a straightforward rectangle would have been boring. A modest curve, or bow, at the front of the deck gives a subtle feeling of standing at the prow of a ship, especially when leaning against the railing and looking out at the yard.

CHOOSING MATERIALS. The decking, railing, and fascia are all made of ipé, an expensive but beautiful choice. The railing is made of cedar, and the posts, beams, joists, and stringers all must be made of treated pine. The most visible elements—the post and the front stringer—are carefully stained to nearly match the color of the stained ipé.

Because all parts of the deck—even its underclothes—would be on display, all the materials needed to be chosen with extra care. With most decks, the framing is covered up, so a good builder chooses lumber that is free of structural defects but doesn't pay much attention to appearance. For this deck, not only did Lea use No. 1 lumber (as he always does), he also selected the individual boards

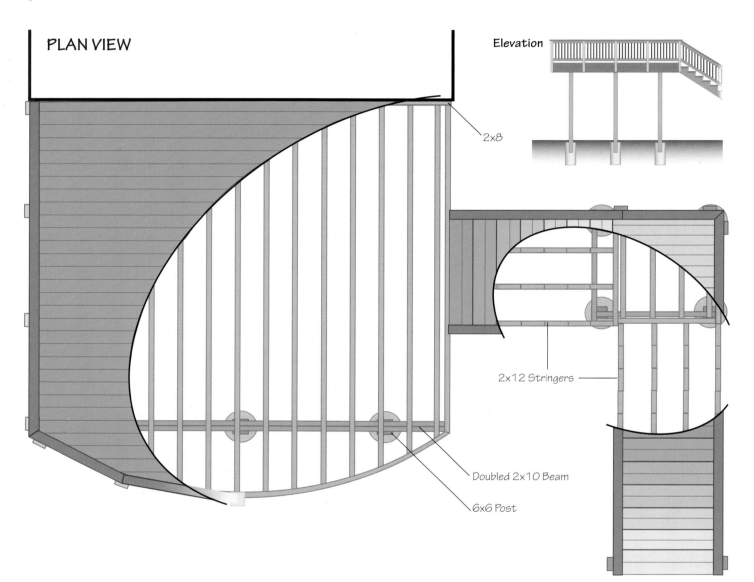

PLAN VIEW

Elevation

2x8

2x12 Stringers

Doubled 2x10 Beam

6x6 Post

MATERIALS USED FOR THIS DECK

Framing (all treated)	6x6 posts 2x8 ledger and joists Doubled 2x10 beams 2x12 stringers	Railing	4x4 cedar posts 2x4 cedar rails Metal balusters with plastic brackets ⁵⁄₄x6 ipé rail cap
Decking and Fascia	⁵⁄₄x6 ipé		

carefully to be sure they were perfectly straight and free of even small cosmetic blemishes.

Because the curve is so gentle, Lea was able to use ipé—perhaps the most difficult of all boards to bend—for the fascia. PVC fascia board, which bends easily, would have been a simpler and less-expensive option, but because the fascia would be so prominently displayed, the owners felt it worth the cost to use ipé instead.

THE RAILING AND STAIRS. The railing posts and rails are made of cedar 4x4 and 2x4, which is easily stained to nearly match the decking. The top rail cap is made of ¾ ipé decking, which is 1 inch thick. This lends a lighter feel than a standard two-by rail cap, and the hardwood is plenty strong and stable. An ogee-shaped detail on either side of the rail cap is made using a router.

DECK AND STAIR RAILINGS offer opportunities for interesting details, emphasized by the routed edges of the rail cap, above left.

THOUGH IT IS AMONG THE MOST EXPENSIVE OF THE TROPICAL HARDWOODS, ipé is often chosen because of its beautiful grain, above right.

IT IS NOT POSSIBLE TO BEND A HARDWOOD to make a curved railing, so the railing instead has a series of straight pieces that join at the posts with slight angles, below. The effect is slightly geometric, but mostly feels like a curve.

CONSTRUCTION TECHNIQUES

A second-story deck presents challenges, so tackle a project like this only if you are experienced, have at least two able helpers, and take plenty of safety precautions.

FRAMING. Lea supports the beam temporarily as he builds the framing and installs the posts and footings later. Use ample temporary braces to hold the supports and the beam firmly in place. Often it works best to attach one brace to the house and install two more angled braces to stakes driven into the ground.

Because the front is curved, you cannot install the header joist until last. Attach the joists to the header using joist hangers, and have them "run wild" past the beam; you will cut them to length later. Attach the joists to the beam using angle-driven screws or anchoring hardware, taking care to keep them a consistent distance apart. On top of the joists, lay a temporary board, and drive screws through it into each joist, to keep the joists from wandering as you work.

FROM THIS ANGLE you can see the under-framing, left. Starting from the outside and working inward are the fascia board, with kerf cuts; the header joist, with kerf cuts; and blocking pieces between the joists, below.

Make a large "compass" out of string or a board, and mark the tops of the joists for cutting at a curve. (See page 76.) Cut each joist.

To make the curved header, cut a series of "kerfs" in the back of the board. Set a circular saw to cut to a depth of about ¾ inch, and cut across the board every 2 inches or so. Once all these kerfs are cut, you will be able to bend the board. Do not cut the header to length. Hold it in position, overhanging at each side, and drive screws to attach the header to each joist. To add strength, cut individual blocking pieces to fit between the joists, and install them behind the header.

THE STAIRWAY. Carefully calculate the height of the landing and the rises and runs of the stairs so that all the steps will end up being the same height and depth. Build a landing, which is basically a small deck; then build stairs to run from the deck to the landing and from the landing to the bottom.

THE RAILING. The railing uses notched 4x4 posts, which are attached to the outside of the stringers. The carriage bolts holding the posts must be long because they run through the post, the fascia, the header, and the blocking piece.

Cut 2x4 top and bottom rails to fit between the posts, but don't install them yet. Drive evenly spaced baluster brackets into the rails; slip on the rails to make a balustrade section; and attach the balustrades to the posts. Attach the rail-cap pieces using stainless-steel screws.

A LANDING is constructed much like a small deck with posts.

AT THE BOTTOM, stringers rest on a concrete foundation, below.

THE STAIR STRINGERS are firmly attached to the deck and landing using bolts, right.

BISCUIT JOINERY

THE PLACE WHERE CAP RAIL PIECES JOIN to make a 90-degree turn is notorious for coming apart over time, resulting in an unattractive gap. One way to limit this problem is to use very stable lumber—say, hardwood, or No. 1 KDAT (kiln-dried after treatment) treated lumber. To further strengthen the joint, use biscuits. You will need a biscuit joiner, polyurethane glue, and some No. 1 biscuits.

1. Cut the two cap rail pieces, and test to make sure they fit. While holding the two pieces together, draw reference lines across the joint so that both pieces are marked for the location of the biscuit cuts. Adjust a biscuit joiner to cut into the center of the rail's thickness; set it to the correct depth for the biscuits you will use; and cut the biscuit holes. Cut holes for both pieces.

2. Attach the first piece. Squirt some glue into the holes, and slip in the biscuits.

3. Squirt glue into the holes of the second piece, and also cover the cut face with a layer of glue.

4. Push the second piece firmly into place. Drill pilot and countersink holes, slightly angled toward the first piece, and drive screws to attach to the post and/or the top rail.

5. If you install plugs, sand them smooth. After a few minutes, the polyurethane glue will ooze out of the joint. Allow a day for it to completely harden; then sand it away, and smooth the surface.

CHIPPENDALE RAILING DESIGN

A "TRUE" CHIPPENDALE RAIL-
ING DESIGN stretches all the way
from post to post. This modified
design is much easier to make and
creates a less busy railing. Once the
Chippendale section is finished, you
can fill in both sides with simple
vertical balusters.

THE FINISHED DESIGN

1. Make a jig: on a piece of plywood,
draw the design you want to create. Attach 2x2 or 1x2 cleats with screws to the
plywood, so they will hold the railing
pieces in place as you work. Cut the two
side pieces to length so that they will fit
between the bottom and the top rails,
and position them on the jig. Measure for
pieces that will fit snugly between the
side pieces.

2. If you are skilled, you can use a hand
miter saw. However, a good-quality and
accurately adjusted power miter saw
makes the work go quickly and produces
precise cuts. Cut the top and bottom
pieces to fit; then cut the center angle
piece, which has a point at each end.

3. Drive nails or screws to attach the
pieces as you go so that they will fit snugly
together. (If you use screws or hand-driven
nails, be sure to drill pilot holes first.) If you
can punch the piece into place with your
hand, you've achieved a good fit. If you
need to pound with a hammer, it is too
tight. Loose fits will develop gaps.

4. Cut and attach the two pieces with a
point at one end. Cut all the smallest
pieces to the same length. Attach with
angle-driven nails; then remove the entire
piece, and drive fasteners through the
sidepieces.

NOSING INTO THE YARD

THIS MODERATELY SIZED DECK STEPS GENTLY UPWARD TO CONFORM
TO THE LANDSCAPE. OPPOSING CURVED SHAPES, TWO HERRINGBONE
DECKING PATTERNS, AND A CURVED BENCH MAKE IT RICH IN DETAIL
WITHOUT BEING VISUALLY BUSY.

THE UPPER LEVEL provides just the right space for a small table with chairs, plus room for kids to run around.

DESIGN CONSIDERATIONS

This backyard was a mess, and the owners wanted to redo both the deck and the landscape. The first step was to demolish an existing one-level treated deck that had become dingy and ugly. Next, they chose a landscaper and a deck builder at the same time. Lea often works with landscapers, and knows both how to design a deck that conforms to the yard and how to coordinate his work with other contractors.

Landscaping decisions often greatly impact the feel and usefulness of a deck. Here, the first decision was to remove a large oak tree, which put the entire site into dense shade for three-quarters of the year. Even with that tree removed, it's still a woody site, but now there's enough open space to produce pleasant, dappled light throughout most of the day.

Having spent some time using a smaller deck, the owners decided they wanted a larger deck, but didn't need a huge one; 600 square feet felt about right. They were also tired of a boring rectangular deck and wanted some interesting design touches.

To cite a cliché that often proves true, form followed function. The yard is only a foot or so below the patio door and slopes gently upward from there, so expanding the deck outward meant they needed to step up the levels. The solution is a curved shape, with the "nose" of the upper curved section extending to the yard's highest point. The back of the upper section could have been straight and parallel with the house, but adding a sort of counter-curve produces an eye-shaped section that comfortably fits a dining table.

PLAN VIEW

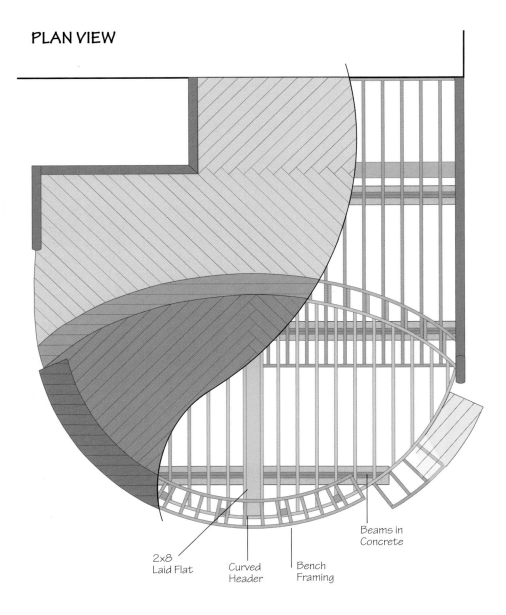

2x8
Laid Flat

Curved
Header

Bench
Framing

Beams in
Concrete

Because the deck is low, no railing is required by code. However, a rail section is used at one end to partially hide the central air conditioning unit; at the other end of the deck, a small railing makes another decorative, short wall. A bench is added to the outer edge of the deck, following the curve, to provide a bit of a barrier. Because it is low, it does not inhibit the view of the yard, and it allows parents to keep an eye on the kids in the yard.

A deck this low to the ground calls for burying the beams in trenches, as described in "Construction Techniques," opposite. This adds some expense; if the lawn allows it, building a foot or so higher would be easier and less costly.

The decking, as well as the fascia and the visible parts of the bench, is made of cambara, a tropical hardwood that at the time of this writing cost a good deal less than ipé. It gains a darker hue after several years of applying sealer.

On a low deck like this, it's important to use high-quality pressure-treated lumber for the framing. Pieces that come near the ground should be labeled "ground contact"; pieces that touch the ground should be rated for "in-ground" use.

MATERIALS USED FOR THIS DECK

Framing (all treated)	Doubled 2x8 beams, set in concrete trenches 2x8 ledger and joists	Benches	4x4 cedar posts 2x4 and 1x4 cedar framing 1x4 cambara trim 5/4x6 cambara seat pieces
Decking and Fascia	5/4x6 cambara		
Railing	4x4 cedar posts 2x4 Cambara rails Metal balusters with plastic brackets		

CONSTRUCTION TECHNIQUES

Gray Beam

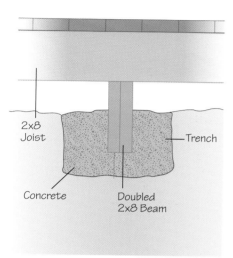

2x8
Joist

Concrete

Trench

Doubled
2x8 Beam

TRENCH-LAID BEAMS. On decks this low, Lea often uses "gray beams," by which he means beams that are set in concrete. On a sloped site, this calls for careful planning because the trenches must all be dug at the correct depth before the framing is built. Lay out for the beam locations, and use a string line level or a water level to determine the height of the beams. Dig trenches that extend four inches below the bottoms of the beams.

At this point, you could temporarily brace the beams at the correct height and pour concrete into the trenches; you will need to wait a day for the concrete to set before installing the framing. Lea prefers to first just set the beams in the trenches, and build the framing—ledger, joists, and blocking—using temporary supports. For this method, use metal straps to attach the beams to the undersides of the joists, and pour the concrete. Again, think ahead: if some joists would get in the way of pouring the concrete, you may

choose to wait and install them after pouring the concrete.

Because this method calls for so much concrete, you may want to order it delivered in a truck. Be sure the concrete meets local codes for strength; 3,000 p.s.i. concrete will probably be fine. You may be required to install metal concrete reinforcing bar under the beams or to add fiberglass reinforcement to the concrete mix.

FRAMING FOR CURVES AND HERRINGBONE DECKING. Install all framing on temporary supports. Start by installing the ledger against the house. Frame the lower level using a straight header joist that will be buried under the step and the upper level of the deck.

Construct the upper level, which is one step up from the lower level. Because this is curved on both sides, framing is tricky. Start with two header joists that are longer than they will end up being. On the back of each header, cut a series of kerfs—cuts about ¾ inch deep—every two inches or so all along the length of the headers. Now you will be able to bend them into curves.

Cut the two center joists to length. To prepare for the herring-bone decking, attach a flat-laid 2x8 between the joists, flush with the tops of the joists. This will provide nailing surface for the herringbone decking.

A HERRINGBONE PATTERN is possible because there is a flat-laid 2x8 that is used for a nailing surface installed down the center of the deck.

Bench

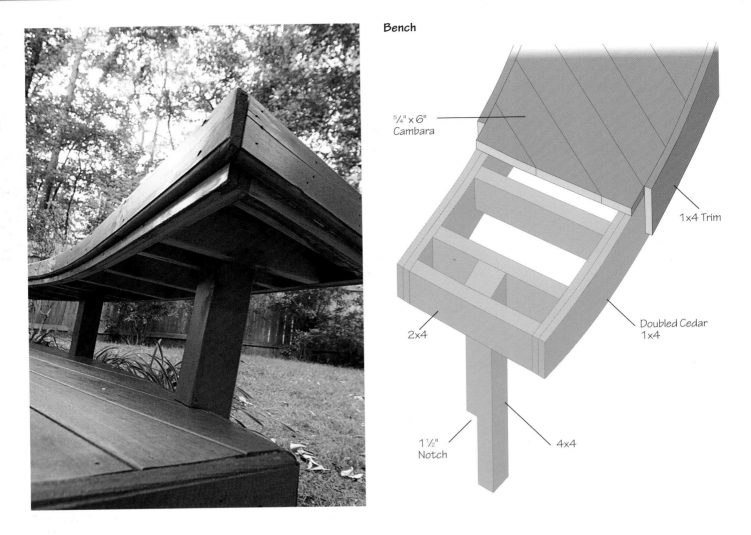

⁵/₄" x 6" Cambara

1x4 Trim

2x4

Doubled Cedar 1x4

1½" Notch

4x4

Attach the joists and flat-laid-piece to the center of the two headers. Working with several helpers, bend the headers to achieve the shape you desire for the upper level. You will need to cut the boards at each end. The rest of the joists must be marked in place and cut one at a time. For a tight fit against the header joists, set your circular saw to cut at a bevel. Hold a board on top of the headers, and mark with a pencil to determine the correct bevel.

Once the upper level is framed and installed on temporary supports, construct framing for the step. Use kerf cuts again to make the headers bendable, and install short joists every 16 inches.

(To install decking with concealed fasteners, see "Sinking and Pugging Screws," page 108.)

THE BENCH. This bench is a basic design, made somewhat more complicated because it has to describe a curve. Install posts against the outside of the deck, every four or five feet. Cut a number of 2x4 crosspieces, 6 inches shorter than the finished width of the bench top. Attach crosspieces to each side of the posts.

You could use kerf-cut 2x4s for the long curved framing pieces, and Lea often does that. Here, he instead uses doubled cedar 1x4s for the curved sides of the bench; the cedar is flexible enough to make the curve without the need for kerf cuts. (You cannot use cedar for the deck framing; it is not sufficiently strong or rot resistant.) Attach them to the crosspieces; then cut them to length. Attach more crosspieces, spaced every 16 inches or so.

Attach decking boards onto the bench framing, allowing it to "run wild" (overhang). Looking at the gaps between the decking boards, carefully mark a curved line, and cut the boards so that they are flush with the curved framing pieces. Add the trim pieces.

THE CURVED BENCH, above left, is a nice detail that can be accomplished with cedar framing. Cut the post about 15 in. long to finish with a seat that is a comfortable height.

LEA USED A ROUTER to add detail to many of the trim pieces, opposite top.

HERRINGBONE PIECES that butt against the house cannot be run wild and cut later; you must carefully measure and cut each decking piece, opposite bottom.

THREE ELEGANT ROOMS

THIS DECK USES SEVERAL CURVED LINES AND THREE LEVELS TO
DEFINE TWO DINING AREAS AND A SPACIOUS LIVING ROOM ORIENTED
TOWARD AN OUTDOOR FIREPLACE. THE DECK IS SO LOW TO THE
GROUND IT SEEMS AS THOUGH IT IS NEARLY A PART OF THE YARD.

DECKSOUTH

DESIGN CONSIDERATIONS

As with many of Lea's jobs, the landscaping went hand in hand with the deck building. Before building the deck, the yard sloped toward the house, causing flooding in the basement during heavy rains. The area near the house was excavated so water would run away, but the yard still sloped upward starting about 20 feet from the house. The owners did not want any steps on the deck, so everything was kept extremely low—so low that not only the beams but also some of the joists are partially buried in the ground.

The owners wanted a fairly formal outdoor space. The cooking area is actually on a separate deck about 20 feet away. This presents a minor inconvenience that they gladly live with in exchange for a deck that can accommodate elegant gatherings as well as informal affairs.

When you walk out the kitchen door, you are on the middle of three levels. On the right is an everyday dining area, with space for a four-chair table. Step up to the upper level, and you find a lovely living room. A tree grows up through the deck here, and a cultured stone fireplace faces the room.

Take two steps down to the lower level, and you are on a nearly rectangular space designed for formal dining. There is plenty of space for an oval six-chair table, positioned well away from the kitchen and near bedroom windows—perfect for languid candlelit meals. Another tree grows up through the decking here.

The decking and fascia are made of ipé, whose rich and varied wood tones are perfect for a formal outdoor space.

IN THE LIVING ROOM, above, chairs can be moved near the fireplace on cool evenings or for close conversation; they can be spaced farther apart for general lounging. The tree is just far enough away from the fireplace so there is no danger of charring the bark.

PLAN VIEW

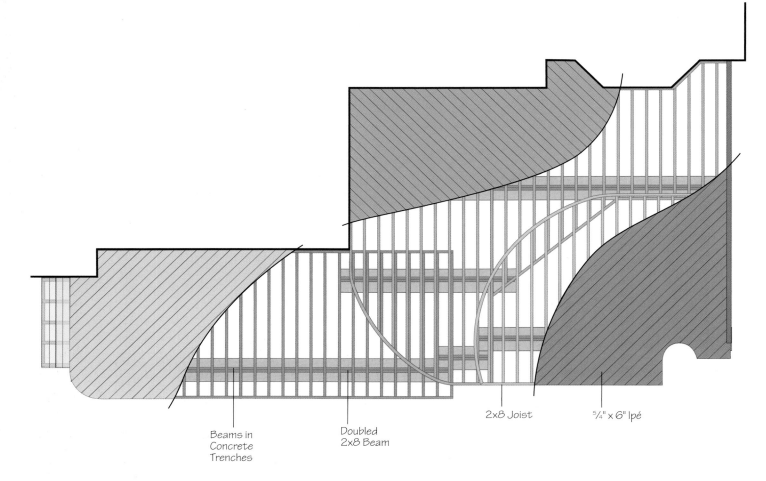

Beams in
Concrete
Trenches

Doubled
2x8 Beam

2x8 Joist

⁵⁄₄" x 6" Ipé

TO CREATE SEPARATE AREAS on what is essentially an open space, Lea uses a couple of design tricks. Here, the house itself helps separate this dining area from the rest of the deck. Other techniques include changing levels, even if only by a step, and changing the direction of the decking.

MATERIALS USED FOR THIS DECK

Framing (all treated)	2x8 ledger and joists Doubled 2x8 beams		Planter	Treated 2x4 framing Treated plywood EPDM liner ⁵⁄₄x6 ipé sides and top trim
Decking and Fascia	⁵⁄₄x6 ipé			
Railing	4x4 ipé posts 2x4 ipé rails and rail cap Metal balusters with plastic brackets			

CONSTRUCTION TECHNIQUES

The beams are buried in concrete-filled trenches, and many of the joists touch the ground as well, so excellent pressure-treated lumber, preferably rated for in-ground use, is definitely called for.

EXCAVATION AND THE LEDGER.
It is very difficult to build in a situation where joists are sunk into the ground; you would need to dig narrow trenches for all those joists. It is best to excavate deep enough so the joists (though perhaps not the beams) are above ground during construction. After the deck is built, soil can be pushed back to partially cover some joists and make the decking nearly level with the ground.

If the house wall has a number of turns like this one, take the time to carefully mark for the ledger height at all points. If the ledger is even ⅛ inch high or low at any point, the decking will not form a smooth surface. Use a laser level, a water level, or work carefully with a regular carpenter's level. Lea is required to bolt his ledgers to the house's framing, but you may be allowed to use screws instead. In any case, provide firm attachment, and flash the ledger area.

Elevation

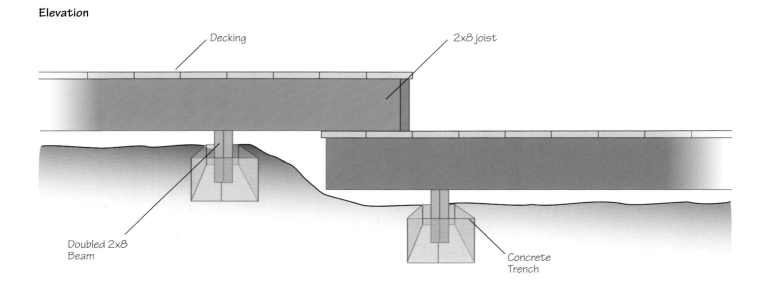

Decking

2x8 joist

Doubled 2x8
Beam

Concrete
Trench

GRAY BEAMS. Beam locations can be tricky on a multilevel deck. When you draw your plan and when you build, start with the lowest level. Once you've figured out where the beam and the joists will go, move on to the next level, then the next. Usually, one level rests on top of another, so you may need fewer beams than you think at first. In this plan, note that the joists attach to a ledger along most of the length, so that one of the beams is short. One of the middle-level beams is very short, supporting a small portion of framing that does not rest on the lower level.

Dig trenches for the beams. Lea uses "gray beams," pouring a trench of concrete after most of the framing is installed; this is described on page 69. Your codes may require other methods. You may need to support the beams every four or five feet with deep concrete footings. Or you may be able to use Lea's technique, which is typically done before the joists are installed.

CURVED FRAMING. To make curved framing at a corner, build with standard rectangular framing, but do not attach the header on the part that will be curved. Tack a board across the

tops of the joists to maintain correct spacing. Make a compass out of a nail, a length of string, and a pencil, as shown below, to mark the tops of the joist where the curve will be.

Making a Curve

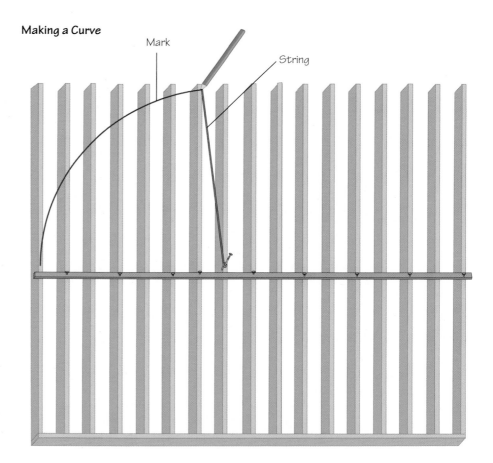

Mark

String

Use a square to draw cut lines on either side of each joist. Cut each joist with a circular saw or small chain saw. (You will need to adjust the saw for a different bevel cut for each joist.) To make a curved header joist, cut a series of ⅜-inch-deep kerfs across the back of a two-by joist, every 2 inches or so; this will make the board flexible. Or use two one-byes if they can be bent to fit.

AROUND A TREE. Frame a simple box around a tree, allowing ample space for the tree to grow in thickness over the next couple of decades. Install the decking so it is fairly tight against the tree. Then use a jigsaw (sabersaw) to cut a curved line around the tree. You may need to recut with the jigsaw every five or six years.

BUILD A FRAMING BOX to surround the tree trunk, right. You can trim the decking to size using a jigsaw. Leave room for growth.

PLANTERS, below, add vertical interest and they can help separate one area from another on the deck.

UPSTAIRS DECK
WITH A COUPLE OF TWISTS

THIS UPPER-LEVEL DECK IS A STRAIGHTFORWARD RECTANGLE, BUT WITH A COUPLE OF DETAILS THAT MAKE IT OUT OF THE ORDINARY: A SPIRAL STAIRCASE AND A PAIR OF LARGE SCALLOPED TRIM PIECES. THE WOODSY MATERIALS GIVE A HOMEY APPEARANCE, AND A SOPHISTICATED HIDDEN DRAINAGE SYSTEM KEEPS THINGS DRY ON THE PATIO BELOW.

DESIGN CONSIDERATIONS

Spiral Stair Elevation

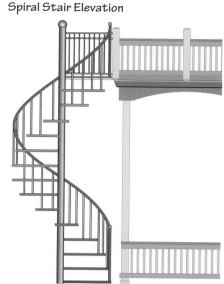

The backyard includes a large patio and pool, as well as a fireplace and plenty of room for cooking and dining. So the deck did not need to carry much of the entertaining load. The customers just wanted a modest space off the upstairs bedroom for relaxing and occasional brunching. They also wanted to provide rain protection for a portion of the patio next to the house.

FRAMING AND WATER PRO-TECTION. The basic deck's construction is straightforward: a ledger, single beam, and rectangular framing. The waterproofing system allows rainwater to seep between the decking boards and flow out to a gutter, which is visible on the front of the deck. Because the gutter is brown, it does not detract from the appearance of the deck.

Once a reliable waterproofing system has been installed, the underside of the deck can be finished much like a porch. Here, a traditional beadboard ceiling is peppered with recessed lights and a pair of ceiling fans. In many areas, a licensed electrician must be hired to install these fixtures. Be sure the electrical fixtures are suitable for outdoor use in your area. In areas with very cold winters or lots of rain, special fixtures may be required.

RAILING AND FINISH MATERIALS. The decking is ipé that the customer chose to leave unsealed so that it turns a rustic gray. The fascia and railing are made of cedar, and the tall structural posts are made of pressure-treated 6x6s, stained to look very similar to the cedar. The trim below the gutter is made of 1x12 boards cut in a scallop design.

The railing is an all-wood design

with an old-fashioned feel. Standard rail posts are used on top, while the lower railing simply attaches to the structural posts.

STAIRCASE. Because the deck is about 8 feet high, a set of wooden steps would need to include a landing, and would take up a lot of room in the yard. The solution: a metal spiral staircase. Such staircases can be ordered to fit from a staircase company. You can choose among a wide range of spiral-stair styles. Here, a relatively inexpensive metal stairway was chosen, but you can add wood treads and other features.

A LITTLE WHIMSY comes in the form of the bird statue at right. The owners placed one on each end post.

A WATERPROOF DECK means you can install recessed lighting and a ceiling fan to light and cool the patio, below.

CONSTRUCTION TECHNIQUES

The basic structure is straightforward, but because the deck is very high and includes a waterproofing system, you should tackle this project only if you have plenty of experience.

FRAMING AND WATERPROOFING. Attach the ledger as required by local codes. Use tall 2x6s or larger boards to temporarily support the joists as you build the framing box. Lea spaces his joists 12 inches on center, but because the decking runs parallel with the house, you could

space them every 16 inches.

Once the framing is complete, install the waterproofing system. See page 51 for more information. Here, a waterproofing membrane is run out the front of the framing; you will install and trim and the gutter later.

Where a patio with a solid concrete slab exists, the posts may be allowed to sit on top of post anchors that are attached to the patio with masonry anchors. Or the inspector may make you cut holes in the patio with a masonry saw; dig and pour footings; and install posts in concrete

as you normally would. You will then need to patch the patio around the posts. Check with your building department for specific requirements.

In Lea's area, footings are made by digging a deep hole—usually, at least 36 inches, or until undisturbed soil is found—and then pouring concrete. The concrete does not come up to the surface, so it is not visible after the post is installed and the hole is backfilled. In some areas, footings are required to rise above the ground; check with local codes.

PLAN VIEW

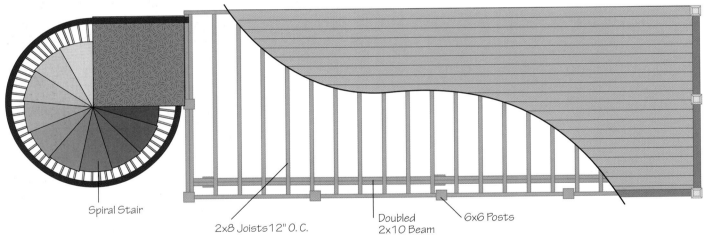

Spiral Stair

2x8 Joists 12" O. C.

Doubled
2x10 Beam

6x6 Posts

MATERIALS USED FOR THIS DECK

Framing (all treated)	6x6 posts 2x8 for ledger and joists Doubled 2x10 for beam
Decking and Fascia	¾x6 ipé decking Cedar 1x12 and 1x8 for fascia and trim
Upper Railing	6x6 cedar posts 2x6 cedar top and bottom rails 2x2 cedar balusters

Lower Railing	2x4 top and bottom rails 2x2 balusters 1x4 rear trim pieces 2x6 rail cap

Waterproofing system, including EPDM sheeting and gutter

Custom-made metal spiral staircase

DECKSOUTH

LEA BUILT THIS RAILING on site. The top and bottom rails are attached to the structural posts.

A RUBBER-LIKE MEMBRANE is installed under the decking and channels water to the gutter system.

THE SCALLOPED DESIGN of the support beam adds a bit of design flair to a standard rectangular deck.

SPIRAL STAIRCASES help to conserve room in a crowded yard. Stair fabricators will design and install the stairs.

DECKING AND RAILING. To build the upstairs railing, Lea notch-cuts the 6x6 posts to bring the railing in a bit and make it feel more a part of the deck. Some codes require 4x4 rail posts to be unnotched, but may allow notching for 6x6s. Install flat-laid 2x6 top and bottom rails. Lea routs the edges using an ogee bit before installing them. Attach 2x2 nailers to the underside of the top rail and the top of the bottom rail, and cut 2x2 balusters to fit between the rails.

For the lower rail, cut 2x4 top and bottom rails, and attach them to the front of the structural posts. Cut and attach 2x2 balusters so that they are flush with the tops and bottoms of the rails. For a finished look, cut 1x4s to fit

between the posts, and attach them to the rear of the balusters, flush with their tops and bottoms. Finish with a 2x4 rail cap. Again, Lea routs the edges of the rail cap before installing.

TRIM FINISHES. Lea uses a variety of trim pieces to finish off the deck. Some must be rip-cut from pieces of 1x8 or 1x12. Some are given a routed edge. To make, cut, and install trim pieces, you will find that a good table saw, power miter saw, and power nailer will make things go faster and produce more professional results.

To mark for cutting the 1x12 scallop pieces, first cut the pieces to length and make sure they fit. Mark where you want the curved cutouts to

begin and end so that the straight sections are all the same length. Place each board on a flat surface, and use a pencil-and-string compass to mark for the curve. For this curve, the compass should be about 10 feet long. You will need to experiment with the length of the string until you achieve a line that creates the desired curve. Cut using a jigsaw (sabersaw).

STAIRCASE. Once the deck is mostly or all built, contact a spiral-staircase maker. They will come out and take measurements, and fabricate and install the unit. Be sure the staircase is firmly attached at both bottom and top, and that the center post lines up visually with the deck's posts.

CLADDING POSTS AND RAILS

TRADITIONAL SOUTHERN ARCHITECTURE often includes richly detailed and layered white trim, especially on posts and railings. Such trim was typically made of high-grade wood that was carefully painted. Maintaining the crisp lines of such trim required frequent meticulous repainting, and after a few decades rotted boards often needed to be replaced. Today, trim made of synthetic materials offers the same look with much lower maintenance. It can be cut precisely, with no splintering. And it resists shrinking and warping, so joints stay tight. Many synthetic materials can be painted.

MATERIAL OPTIONS

A variety of synthetic trim materials are available. Builders often refer to it by the name of the manufacturer, and the material itself will have a long-winded chemical name, perhaps shortened to PVC or PVA. Check with your supplier to find the type that performs well in your area. Also check to see if the material will accept paint. In general, if the surface is glossy, it should not be painted; if it has a matte finish, it can be painted. Many of Lea's clients choose a matte finish and leave it unpainted—they just prefer a less shiny surface.

Nowadays it's not unusual to combine natural and synthetic materials. White posts and trim contrast nicely with natural wood of most any hue. On the deck shown below, white PVC covers the posts and the fascia; and trim pieces are layered over the wrapping for a stately appearance. The ipé decking looks handsome next to it.

APPLYING SYNTHETIC CLADDING AND TRIM

Where you need to bend a piece that will be tight against a board, look for "fascia board," which is about ½ inch thick. Synthetic cladding and trim boards are about ¾ inch thick to mimic the look and stiffness of one-by lumber. (These boards cannot be used to provide structural support to a deck, but they will feel just as strong as wood when used as trim.)

The posts and other materials that you clad will almost certainly not be perfectly straight, but the cladding can come very close to perfection. When cladding, you will create a box whose inside is an inch or two larger than the members being covered. This not only allows you to straighten things out but also creates channels where an electrician can run cables for lights and fans. Also, make sure that the cladding will clear any protruding fasteners.

A power finishing nailer is the tool of choice for attaching synthetic trim. Hand nailing will cause pieces to shake as you work, and screws—even finishing screws—have heads that leave noticeable holes.

Start by carefully checking the member to be clad. If you find a perfectly straight side with no protruding fasteners, attach the first piece tight against that side, and work from there. If no side is perfect, use shims to attach the first piece, carefully checking for straightness as you go.

Once a post is wrapped, attach any railings or other wood pieces that will butt against it. Then apply synthetic trim pieces.

WRAPPING POSTS AND RAILS in PVC accomplishes a few goals: it provides a crisp, clean appearance; the material cuts down on maintenance; and the channels allow you to run wiring while keeping it out of sight.

ANOTHER FINE POINT

LEA LIKES TO MAKE THE JOINT between decking and house as tight a possible—not only for appearance sake, but to make it easier to sweep and clean the deck. Against a brick house, Lea rip-cuts hardwood pieces to the size of 1x2s and carefully trims out the joint between decking and wall. If the wall is stucco, he uses a masonry blade to carefully cut out a channel in the stucco to hold the decking.

LONG AND TALL

ON AN ALREADY IMPRESSIVE PATIO WITH A LARGE POOL, A SMALL
UPPER-LEVEL DECK WOULD HAVE BEEN FINE. BUT THE OWNERS THREW
CAUTION TO THE WIND AND BUILT AN IMPOSING STRUCTURE THAT
MAKES THEIR BACKYARD STUNNING. NOW, PEOPLE CAN ENJOY THE
LOWER LEVEL EVEN DURING A RAINSTORM, AND THE NEW UPSTAIRS
PROVIDES A LOVELY PLACE TO EAT AND GAZE AT THE VIEW.

DESIGN CONSIDERATIONS

Actually, practical considerations were part of the reason for this large upstairs deck. The only upstairs door, leading to a living area, is at the far end. A small deck could have been put there, with a set of stairs connecting to the patio. But then the pathway leading out to the front of the house would have meandered down to the patio, around, and up another set of stairs. A lengthy deck with stairs at the other end that wrap around provides a nice path that is separate from the patio area.

Also, the owners were interested in gaining a good-size area with shelter from the rain. Because there was no room to build outward, a long water-proofed deck was a logical solution.

The position of the pool pretty much determined that the deck would be about 8 feet wide; any more would have put the posts too close to the pool. A large bay window in the middle naturally divides the deck into two usable areas. One area, near the house, is fairly narrow but large enough for a table with chairs. The other area, at the corner near the stairs, is more spacious. So they decided to put a pergola there to provide dappled shade and add some architectural lines.

Most of the visible portions of the deck—posts, railings, fascia, and trim—are covered with knotty cedar, stained a pleasingly homey brown. This may seem a surprising choice for the house, which has so many large windows and so much trim that the overall effect is classical rather than homey. With all those clean, painted lines, a composite deck would have blended in better. But the owners wanted to make a splash rather than blending in. And the cedar fits naturally with the stonework below, so it actually provides a graceful transition to the patio.

THE OVERALL DIMENSIONS of the deck are determined by the location of the pool and the patio below. The size of the decking area means that the space can accommodate two separate living areas and a pergola for some upper-level shade.

CONSTRUCTION TECHNIQUES

On a deck this large, you might think it best to set the posts first, and build on top of them. But Lea finds it best to build the deck on temporary supports, and then install the posts later. That way, he can be sure that the posts are all straight and perfectly aligned with the framing.

FRAMING AND POSTS. This deck does not have the usual beam positioned under the joists. Instead, it uses a "flush beam": the header joists

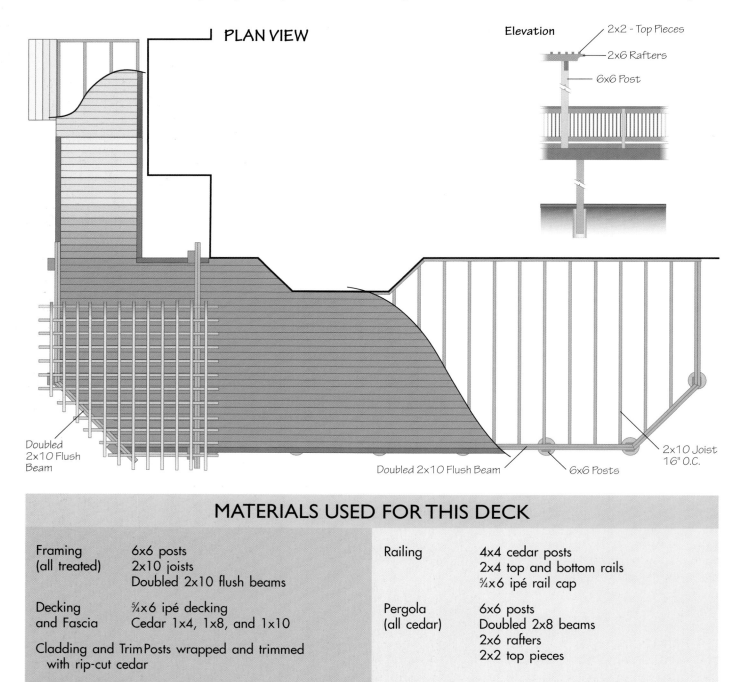

PLAN VIEW

Elevation

2x2 - Top Pieces
2x6 Rafters
6x6 Post

Doubled
2x10 Flush
Beam

Doubled 2x10 Flush Beam

6x6 Posts

2x10 Joist
16" O.C.

MATERIALS USED FOR THIS DECK

Framing (all treated)	6x6 posts 2x10 joists Doubled 2x10 flush beams		Railing	4x4 cedar posts 2x4 top and bottom rails ⁵⁄₄x6 ipé rail cap
Decking and Fascia	⁵⁄₄x6 ipé decking Cedar 1x4, 1x8, and 1x10		Pergola (all cedar)	6x6 posts Doubled 2x8 beams 2x6 rafters 2x2 top pieces
Cladding and Trim	Posts wrapped and trimmed with rip-cut cedar			
Scallop pieces from cedar 1x12				

are doubled, to make them into beams, and the joists are joined to the beam using joist hangers. This arrangement is common when the underside of the deck needs to be smooth, to accommodate a drainage system.

To make a flush beam, first build and temporarily support the framing box—the ledger, the header, and the outside joists. At the angled corners, use 45-degree bevel cuts. Then add a "sister" joist to the side of the headers to create a beam. Drive plenty of nails or screws in a regular pattern so that the two two-byes become essentially one piece of lumber. For extra strength, sister the outside joists.

The patio stones rest on a solid concrete slab, but the inspector did not consider the slab strong enough to support the deck. Lea used a masonry saw to cut holes in the patio, dig the holes, and pour footings.

CLADDING AND TRIM. On a deck with plenty of wrapping and trim, take your time to determine the order in which you will install the boards. You'll need a table saw to rip-cut lots of boards, and a power miter saw to cut lots of miters. Buy the highest-quality and driest cedar to minimize shrinkage and warping that would lead to open joints.

Once the decking is installed, cover the outside and header joists, then the posts with cedar one-by boards. Cut scallop trim pieces out of 2x12s to fit between the posts. Just below the scallop boards, create a newel-like effect by installing 2-inch-wide trim pieces, then 1-inch wide pieces below. To trim the bottom of the posts, use a router with an ogee bit to make a board that looks somewhat like inside base.

THE PERGOLA. It helps if you draw a layout of the pergola's roof. First cut the posts all to the same height, and notch them for the beams which are made of doubled 2x8s. Because

boards vary a bit in thickness and width, hold two 2x8s together and measure to determine the dimensions of the notches. Bolt the posts in place, and work carefully with a helper so that you don't bump the posts as you install the rest of the pieces. Cut the beams to size, and laminate them together. Bolt the

beams to the posts. Evenly space the 2x6 rafters on top of the beams, and attach them by drilling pilot holes and angle-driving screws or nails into the beams. Cut and install 2x2 top pieces, again spacing them evenly over the pergola surface; attach with a single screw or nail at each joint.

ROUTING THE RAIL

WHEN USING A ROUTER to create a detailed or rounded edge, select an edging bit that is guaranteed not to dig in too deep. Test on scrap pieces, and adjust the depth of the bit until you achieve the desired effect. Hold the router with its base flat on the board and the bit an inch or so away. Turn on the router; move the bit into the board; and hold the base-plate firmly flat as you either push or pull the router. Move in the direction of most resistance, so the router does not skip away. If you make a mistake, you can probably just go over the spot again.

THE CEDAR PERGOLA provides some shade itself, but once covered with climbing plants, it will offer a cool spot to relax.

FINE DECKS, INC.

Clemens Jellema
Fine Decks, Inc.
Owings, MD
(410) 286-9092
www.finedecks.com

FINE DECKS, INC.

Clemens Jellema (pronounced "Yellema") runs Fine Decks, Inc., a medium-sized operation in the Baltimore/D.C. area. He typically keeps three crews busy building decks and spends most of his time designing and supervising rather than building himself.

Most of Jellema's customers want decks with a finished appearance that they can show off; they are not interested in "rustic" or "woodsy." He offers decks with smooth surfaces and hardly any visible fastener heads. Like many people around the country, his customers would like a low-maintenance deck, but many are willing to pay for yearly cleaning and staining in exchange for the beauty of Brazilian hardwood.

PRODUCING A DESIGN

Most designs start with a rough sketch made at the customer's home. Then Jellema likes to go home to his office where he spends hours playing around with a deck design software program. Such a program is probably too expensive for a homeowner, but it allows a professional deck builder to quickly experiment with various sizes and configurations.

THIS SMALL DECK, which includes a pergola, right, anchors the end of a swimming pool. Besides being a focal point in the yard, the dappled shade provides some relief from the heat.

SCREENED-IN PORCHES, above, increase the functionality of a deck. The owners made the most of this design by adding a spa to the enclosed area.

GOOD DECK DESIGNERS tend to create decks that follow the natural contours of the land, right. The levels shown here lend themselves to separate activity areas.

JELLEMA LIMITS THE SIZE of his decks so they don't overpower the facade of the house. Still, many decks are in the 400- to 500-square-foot range.

COMPUTER DESIGN. Many builders make and present their plans with simple pencil drawings, which can be fine as long as you gain a good idea of how the deck will look on your yard. However, some builders like Jellema have mastered the use of special design software that actually "builds" a virtual deck. Once the deck is created, it can be looked at on the screen from every possible angle to give a more realistic view of traffic flow, the size of various areas, and the deck's appearance. Finish materials can be changed with the press of a few keys. You can even place furniture and planters on the deck. If you spin the deck around and look from behind, you can get a good idea of how the deck and its railings will affect the view of the yard when looking from inside your house.

A great advantage of programs like this is that you can easily experiment with design alternatives. If for example, you are considering adding a second decking level, the program can quickly show it, and tell you how much new material you will need so the builder can tally the cost.

OVERALL SIZE. Jellema feels that the best-looking decks stay within the dimensions of the house, meaning that they generally occupy about 80 percent of the house's rear wall. The houses in Jellema's area tend to be large, so many of his decks are a spacious 400 to 500 square feet.

ROOMS AND PATHS. Most decks are divided into specific areas: a dining area at least 12 feet square; a relaxing area at least 10 × 12 feet; and a grilling area at least 10 feet square. The dining area may vary in size depending on the table and chairs to be used. The relaxing area may accommodate two Adirondack chairs or a couple of lounge chairs with a small table between. Jellema thinks it

MOST DECKS are divided into separate activity areas. Although compact, this spot is perfect for relaxing in the sun after a dip in the pool at the top of the stairs.

WRAPPING BEAMS AND POSTS

ON THIS WOOD DECK, Jellema has wrapped a post and beam with ipé decking. This adds a touch of grace even when the pressure-treated joists are also visible.

FOR A FINISHED APPEARANCE, Jellema wraps exposed beams and other structural members in composite material. The wood beams here are encased in the same material as used for the railings and decking.

important that the grilling area be about 12 to 16 feet away from the dining area—not so close that the smoke bothers people but close enough for easy transport of food.

If a set of stairs leads to the yard, Jellema states that there should be a clear walkway from the patio door to the stairs. This pathway should not infringe on the areas designated for dining, grilling, or relaxing.

DECKING AND RAILING DETAILS.
Jellema usually installs unnotched railing posts outside the deck's header and outside joists. This makes the most of a deck's square footage. On large decks, he may install the railing posts inside the framing, producing a subtly cozy feel that some people prefer.

Wherever possible, he avoids decking seams (a.k.a. "butt joints"), which are somewhat unattractive and tend to come apart over the years. To do this, he often divides a deck surface into visible sections.

A SMALL DECORATIVE FEATURE becomes a focal point on this deck. See it in context of the whole deck in the photo on page 89. Notice how it comes into view for anyone descending the stairs.

MATERIAL CHOICES

Though a growing number of customers opt for maintenance-friendly composites and vinyl decking and railings, ipé, a Brazilian hardwood, is also a common choice. Ipé has such a beautiful grain and natural feel that many people feel it's worth the extra trouble of maintaining it. Jellema recommends a certain deck cleaning company in his area. Because of their relationship, the cleaner is motivated to do an extra-good job when cleaning and staining Jellema's decks.

COST CONSIDERATIONS. At the time this book was written, an ipé deck typically cost $45–$55 per square foot; composite ran $40–$45, and a pressure-treated deck was between $25–$32. A house's deck can greatly impact its resale value. A treated deck typically adds only 40 percent of the value that an ipé or composite deck adds.

FINISH OPTIONS. Most people choose to apply a deck stain/sealer, which comes in a range of colors and emphasizes the grain. Once stained, ipé must be restained yearly. Others choose to leave the ipé unstained so that in time it turns a subtle and slightly shiny silvery gray. A gray deck must be cleaned yearly, or it will take on a dingy appearance.

One of the things that contributes to the price tag of an ipé deck is the labor involved. Many of Jellema's customers opt to the have the fasteners sunk below the surface and then plugged for a neat appearance. This process takes extra time and does increase the cost of the deck, but many customers feel the results are worth the price.

Natural wood looks great against a brick or wood-sided wall, but Jellema feels it looks out of place next to vinyl siding. Most of his composite decks are built against vinyl-sided houses.

Often he installs PVC fascia on an ipé deck. This provides a pleasing contrast in color. Plus, PVC can be bent easily into curves, unlike ipé, so it is sometimes the only fascia that will work.

THE RAIL CAP above provides an opportunity for a deck builder to show off his handiwork. Here, hardwood caps are neatly joined and fastened with counterbored-and-plugged screwheads.

THE DESIGN SOFTWARE that Jellema uses allows him to add planters and benches, below, to his design to see how they work with the overall concept.

INEXPENSIVE BUT NOT CHEAP

MANY DECK BUILDERS BUILD BOTH CUSTOM DECKS (the type featured in this book) and decks that are plainer and less expensive. If you want a modest deck, a general builder may offer a cheap price, but often you can hire a real deck builder to construct a much better deck for only a modest additional cost. In fact, a deck builder will often be less costly than a general contractor.

Jellema, for instance, has a sort of side business building inexpensive decks for town homes and condos. These decks are priced to sell, but are definitely a cut above the cookie-cutter decks that are so often tacked onto new housing. They include many basic features of his more expensive decks, so they will last longer than a deck built by a general contractor, plus they add a few modest details, so they are not simple rectangles. A typical 18- x 12-foot deck with two angled corners and a railing will cost from $5,000 (for treated lumber) to $6,000 (for ipé).

JELLEMA'S TECHNIQUES

■ All of Jellema's structural posts are 6x6s, even if the deck is low and 4x4s would suffice. The post is notched to accommodate the beam, which is typically made of two 2x10s laminated together.

■ His framing usually includes a ledger, attaching the framing to the house, plus a beam running alongside the house, about a foot from the ledger. This "second" beam (most decks have a single beam, supporting the framing away from the house) makes the deck extra strong. Because of the second beam, the ledger can be attached simply with lag screws driven into the house's framing, rather than bolts.

■ To protect the house from rot at the ledger attachment, Jellema cuts away the siding, then installs two flashings: a wide, flat piece of vinyl next to the house, plus a piece of copper flashing that hangs over the ledger.

SUNK-AND-PLUGGED FASTENERS

DOUBLE HEADER JOISTS

NOTCHED POST

■ Around the perimeter of the framing, he uses doubled out-side and header joists. This is not required, but it makes the perimeter stiffer, so the railing posts, which are attached to it, are firmer.

■ Even where it is not required, Jellema usually spaces his joists 12 inches apart, rather than the more usual 16 inches. This adds somewhat to the materials cost but makes for a stronger deck.

COPPER FLASHING

■ He also uses reduced spans or larger lumber than is required. For instance, where code says it's OK to have a 2x6 joist span a distance of 9 feet, Jellema will beef up the framing by using a 2x8 instead or by building with a span of only 7 feet.

■ Although it is time-consuming and adds to the cost of a deck, sinking the decking and railing screws below the surface and filling the resulting holes with wood plugs is a feature most of Jellema's customers choose for their decks. The result of the process is a furniture-like appearance for the deck.

DECK PLUS ISLAND

THIS DESIGN ADDS AN EXTRA PLATFORM JUST OFF THE MAIN DECK. IT IS WITHIN SPEAKING DISTANCE, BUT WITH A BIT OF SECLUSION. A RAILING MAKES THE MAIN DECK FEEL LIKE A ROOM, WHILE THE LOW-LYING PLATFORM FEELS MORE LIKE A PART OF THE YARD. COMPOSITE DECKING AND RAILINGS PRESENT CLEAN LINES THAT BLEND WELL WITH THE HOUSE'S SIDING.

DESIGN CONSIDERATIONS

The yard in front of the main deck is a plain lawn, while the area beyond the lower platform (to the left in the photo) is a small wooded lot. This deck provides a clearly defined space for cooking and dining, as well as a small space that noses into the woods.

TWO DIFFERENT SPACES. The main deck is treated much like an outdoor room, with the railing providing partial "walls." Diners and cooks can easily see into the yard, but the "walls" provide a sense of enclosure. A small bump-out section houses a barbecue unit. It is positioned a few steps from the kitchen door, and six or seven steps away from the dining table—far enough to keep smoke away from diners.

A SMALL ALCOVE, top, provides a handy spot to place a grill. It's a minor addition, but it makes it difficult for someone to accidently touch the hot grill hood.

THE SIDE STAIRS, below, give someone on that side of the yard a clear path to the door of the house. Note how the area to the left of the stairs is just large enough to hold a table and chairs.

A LOW-LEVEL PLATFORM adds space that can be configured for a number of different uses. There are no railings, but the small bench does provide a sense of enclosure. When building on multiple levels, Jellema often runs decking on one level at an angle to the decking on another.

FRAMING IS BUILT AND TEMPORARILY SUPPORTED as you go. A typical temporary support is made with a vertical 2x6 resting on a short 2x6 on the ground. Nail or screw the support to the side of the framing member, and add a cleat just under the member for added strength.

The owners needed two stairways, so they could have easy access to the front and back doors.

The lower island has a small bench and no railing. The bench is oriented toward the main house but provides no impediment for enjoying the yard.

COLOR SCHEME AND PATTERN.

Jellema often installs decking border pieces that are different in color and run around the perimeter of the deck. Here, it was felt that the white railing and fascia board provided enough contrast and variation, so there is no decking border.

When choosing a synthetic decking color, collect as many samples as possible, and hold them up against the house's siding. Get an idea of how they will look together in the sun, in the shade, and at night when the lights are on. Here, the tan-colored decking contrasts, but doesn't clash, with the house's siding.

PLAN VIEW

FINE DECKS, INC.

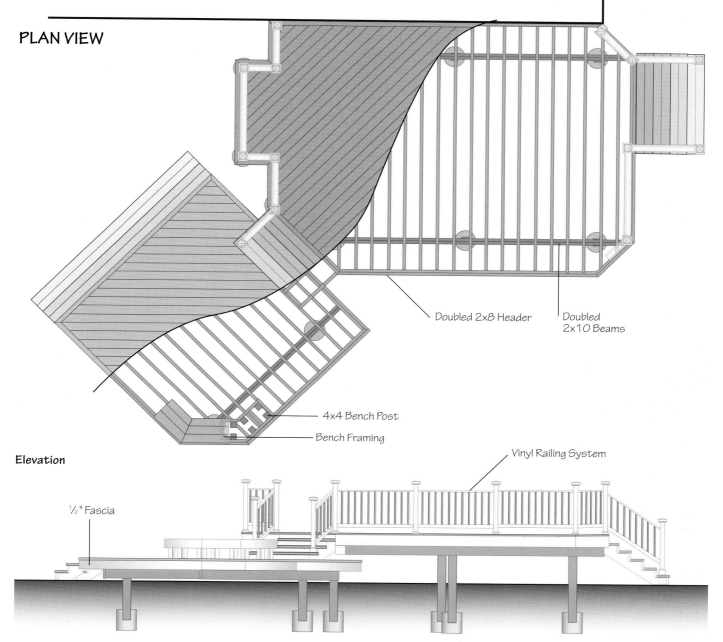

Doubled 2x8 Header

Doubled
2x10 Beams

4x4 Bench Post

Bench Framing

Vinyl Railing System

Elevation

½" Fascia

MATERIALS USED FOR THIS DECK

Framing (all treated)	6x6 posts 2x8 ledger and joists Doubled 2x10 beams 2x12 stair stringers	
Decking and Fascia	⁵⁄₄x6 composite decking ½-in. fascia board	
Railing	Treated 4x4 posts Vinyl railing system	
Bench	Treated 4x4 posts Treated 2x4 framing Composite vinyl to cover all surfaces	

CONSTRUCTION TECHNIQUES

TO INSTALL THE LEDGER, Jellema first removes the siding and installs vinyl flashing material. The installer is marking the ledger for joist locations.

TO MAKE THE DECK MORE RIGID, Jellema doubles up the outside joists. This is not required by most local codes, but it does provide added strength to the deck structure.

For the lower deck especially, be sure to use treated lumber rated for ground contact or in-ground use whenever the boards will come near or into contact with the ground.

LEDGER AND FIRST FLASHING.

Ledgers are installed and flashed in many different ways, depending on local codes and the type of wall to which you are attaching the ledger. Be sure to get the approval of an inspector. The method shown here is fairly standard for houses with vinyl siding.

Remove vinyl siding at least 4 inches above the ledger. Attach heavy duty vinyl flashing to the house. Here, 18-inch-wide flashing is shown. Slip it under the siding, and attach it with nails that are at least 3 inches higher than the ledger; these nails will later be covered when the replacement siding is cut to fit and attached.

Mark the ledger for the joist locations. Then drive screws or bolts as required by your codes. Angle the fasteners slightly upward as they travel into the house so that any collected water will flow down and away from the house. You will install another piece of flashing later, after the joists are installed.

FRAMING BOX AND POSTHOLES.

Starting at one end, work with a helper or two to attach the perimeter framing pieces, or the "framing box"—the outside joists, the headers, and the angled pieces. Temporarily support each piece, checking for level and square as you go. After you have installed several perimeter pieces, go back and recheck; you will likely need to make corrections.

With the basic box built, you can measure for and dig the footing holes.

SOME PROS prefer to build the decking structure on temporary supports and then add the support beams.

POSTS ARE HEAVY, so you may need to have two people hold them in place while another drills holes for the bolts. A clamp helps keep the post in position but will not support its weight.

If the deck is high enough, you may wait until all the interior joists are installed to do this.

Your building department will require postholes to be dug at a required depth. The holes should reach "undisturbed soil" that has not been excavated.

JOISTS AND BEAMS. Add the inside joists, spaced every 12 or 16 inches, depending on the type of decking and whether or not it will run at an angle to the joists. Attach with joist hangers at the ledger, and backnail at the outside joists.

Jellema then adds "sister" joists to double up the outside and header joists for extra strength.

The beams are made of two two-by boards fastened together. Cut the first board to length, and attach it to the underside of the joists using 2x2 cleats to hold it in place. Cut the second board, and attach it to the first by driving 3-inch screws or nails in a grid pattern.

POSTS. Cut the posts to length so they will hang down into the hole the

required distance. Jellema installs them so they are 10 inches above the bottom of the hole. Cut a notch at the top so it fits around the beam. Attach with lag bolts or screws.

You'll probably need to have the local building inspector approve the

footing and post setup at this point.

Check to make sure the post is plumb; then pour the required amount of concrete. Jellema pours enough to reach the bottom of the post, then adds one more 80-pound bag of concrete mix.

JELLEMA MIXES CONCRETE in a heavy-duty plastic bag, and pours it into the hole. He finds this method easier and less messy than mixing in a wheelbarrow or a power mixer.

AT AN OBSTRUCTION, such as a gutter downspout, provide adequate nailing surface for attaching the decking. Often, the solution is to add blocking pieces that fit snugly between joists.

THE FINAL STEP in the flashing system is the application of copper flashing. Jellema uses copper nails to hold the flashing in place.

THE SECOND FLASHING. For the second piece of flashing, Jellema uses a strip of copper that is crimped down the middle. The vertical section of flashing should be at least 3 inches high, so water cannot seep upward and behind it. Hold it in place with copper nails. (Other nails will corrode when in contact with copper.)

Install the decking on top of the flashing. Once the decking is installed, cut the replacement siding piece to fit, and attach. Some builders like to leave a gap of an inch or so under the siding and above the decking, while others install it tight to the decking.

The bench is framed with 4x4 posts with 2x4s between them. Jellema installs some of the posts attached to the framing before the decking is installed. After the decking is run, clad the seat of the structure and the tops with decking pieces.

STAIR FRAMING. Cut notched stringers to run from the upper deck to the lower deck, and from the upper deck to the ground. For the long steps on the lower deck, build box style rather than using stringers.

DECKING, FASCIA, AND RAILING. Install 4x4 treated railing posts inside the framing; then install the decking around the posts. You will need to add blocking pieces to provide nailing surfaces all around the posts. This decking comes with a hidden fastener system. With other types, you will need to drive screws.

A vinyl railing system is a kit with all the parts you need—post sleeves, top and bottom rails, balusters, connectors, and trim pieces. Follow the manufacturer's instructions to cut and assemble the parts.

FINE DECKS, INC.

THIS SET OF STAIRS uses notched stringers to support the risers and treads. For two steps, build one box on top of the other.

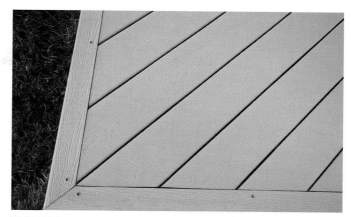

THE DECKING IS INSTALLED using a hidden fastener system; the border is fastened with screws.

BENCHES provide a sense of enclosure and a perch from which to enjoy the scenery. The underlying structure of this bench consists of 4x4 posts covered with decking material. Some of the posts are attached to the joists under the deck.

OUT-OF-THE-BOX RAILING SYSTEMS can speed installation. Usually, kits contain everything you need for the entire railing-and-post system, including trim pieces.

LOW AND SLEEK

THOUGH IT HAS TWO CLEARLY DEFINED ROOMS AND IS MEDIUM IN
OVERALL SIZE, A FEW ANGLES AND SOME LONG STEPS MAKE THIS DECK
SEEM LIKE A LONG RAMBLER. CAREFUL ATTENTION TO WOODWORKING
DETAILS CREATES AN ARTS AND CRAFTS-STYLE DECK—ELEGANT AND
INFORMAL AT THE SAME TIME.

THE AMPLE LOUNGING AREA is located off of the living room. The owners use it as an extension of the interior space. The color of the ipé decking and the mahogany flooring inside help tie the two spaces together.

DESIGN CONSIDERATIONS

In practical terms, the goal here was to enlarge the home's entertaining area and its kitchen. Essentially, two decks accomplish this.

ENTERTAINING AND LOUNGING. Here (on the left in the photo at left), the goal was to blend the deck with the house and the yard. Behind a set of wide French doors is a living room with fairly dark mahogany flooring. Outside, the lawn is woody, with several large trees providing shade much of the time.

Both the design and the materials accomplish a natural transition. The ipé decking is distinct in appearance from the interior mahogany flooring, but similar in spirit, with rich grain and several hues. The owners have children and dogs, and they appreciate the hardwood's resistance to scratching and denting.

Two steps at the French doors and one wraparound step where the deck meets the lawn allow the deck to blend seamlessly with both the inside and the outside.

COOKING AND DINING DECK. The dining table area is a few steps off the kitchen, and a bump-out section for a barbecue grill is a few steps from there, creating a design triangle between kitchen door, table, and grill. The barbecue is a respectable distance of 6 feet or so away from the diners.

THIS DINING TABLE is located near the grill but far enough away so that people are not bothered by the smoke.

CONSTRUCTION TECHNIQUES

PLAN VIEW

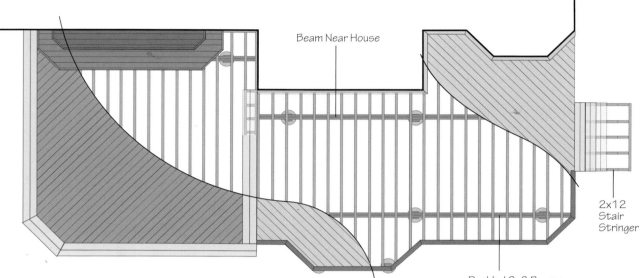

Beam Near House

2x12 Stair Stringer

Doubled 2x8 Beams

Elevation

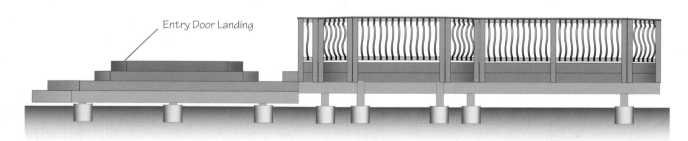

Entry Door Landing

MATERIALS USED FOR THIS DECK

		Railing	4x4 ipé posts
Framing (all treated)	6x6 posts		2x4 ipé top and bottom rails
	2x8 ledger and joists		⁵⁄₄x6 ipé cap rail
	Doubled 2x8 beams		Metal balusters
	2x12 stair stringers		
Decking and Fascia	⁵⁄₄x6 ipé decking		

A low deck like this is fairly easy to construct. However, some of the details—the rail posts at 45-degree corners, the graspable handrail, the tight-to-the-house decking, and the perfectly aligned stairs—call for good carpentry skills. Sinking and plugging the visible fasteners takes a good deal of time and patience.

FRAMING. Be sure to use treated lumber rated for ground contact wherever a beam comes within a few inches of the ground. Here (and for all of Jellema's decks), we show in-ground structural posts, which are commonly used throughout much of the country. However, in your area, aboveground posts may be required.

You will essentially frame for two separate decks and build the steps separately. Attach the ledgers for each of the deck levels, following local codes for flashing it or holding it away from the house. Where there will be two steps leading from the house to the deck, position the ledger that distance below the threshold,

taking into account the thickness of the decking.

Jellema adds extra beams near the house, but your codes may allow you to skip these because the ledger is often considered strong enough to support the deck. Measure and dig holes for the footings.

Construct the framing boxes—the outside and header joists. At the 45-degree angled corners, cut the boards using your circular set for a 22½-degree bevel. Install one board at a time, checking for level and temporarily supporting as you go. Attach the boards with as few fasteners as possible. Check that you are maintaining fairly accurate 90- and 45-degree angles. You will not be perfect. Once the box is completed, check again for level and for accurate angles; make adjustments as needed; and drive in more fasteners.

Lay out for and install the joists, using joist hangers at the ledger and backnailing at the headers. Once this is done, Jellema likes to double up the outside and header joists for extra

strength. This is an especially good idea where there will be railing posts; the extra board will keep them from wobbling.

THE STEPS. You can build the framing for the long steps against the house before or after you install the decking. Either way, double-check your measurements to make sure you will end up at the correct height and that the steps will have the same rise dimension.

The long wraparound step is framed separately. You may need to support it with 4x4 posts, set it on a concrete slab, or rest it on a gravel bed. Construct the small set of steps near the dining area using standard stringers.

DECKING. To avoid butt joints, carefully measure and calculate how many boards of various lengths you will need. If you cannot get enough boards that are long enough, you may need to change the angle or settle for some butt joints.

FINE DECKS, INC.

IPÉ, left, like some other Brazilian hardwoods, is so dense that it has an "A" fire rating—the same as for concrete and steel—so there is no reason to worry about putting a fire pit on it.

A DECKING BORDER, above, is installed against the house. Jellema pushes it tight, but in your area it may be better to leave a gap so that debris and moisture can fall through.

SINKING AND PLUGGING SCREWHEADS

COUNTERSINKING AND PLUGGING IS A TIME-CONSUMING PROCESS, but you can do it if you have the patience and basic carpentry skills. Buy all the plugs you need—hundreds, likely—made of the same material as the decking.

1. Lay the decking in place, and mark for the fastener locations. The straighter the line, the better it will look, but you will probably not achieve perfection. You may need to drive a few finishing nails to keep the boards in place.

2. First, drill a shallow hole the same width as the plugs. Attach a stop to the drill bit, as shown, so you will drill only about ⅜ in. deep.

3. In each hole, drill a pilot hole that is slightly narrower than the screw's shank.

4. Drive decking or stainless-steel screws to fasten the decking to the framing.

5. Squirt a dab of exterior glue into the hole, and tap in the plug.

6. Allow the glue to dry; then sand the plugs flush with the surface. You may need to first use a belt sander, then an orbital sander.

FINE DECKS, INC.

FASCIA AND RAILING. Here, the decking is cut flush to the outside of the header and outside joists, and the fascia is brought up flush with the decking surface. This makes a very nice appearance, but use it only if you are absolutely confident in your carpentry skill and if you are certain your decking and fascia will not warp or shrink, leading to ugly open joints. The joint must remain tightly closed, or the effect will not be appealing. The more common method is to overhang the decking about 1½ inches beyond the joists, and then tuck the fascia under the decking.

Cut and bolt railing posts so that they are the same height; you will need two posts at every angled corner. Cut and attach 2x4 top and bottom rails; then add ⁵⁄₄x6 rail cap for a generous-size railing cap. Screw the metal balusters to the top and bottom rails. The curved balusters used here present a distinctive design touch to the railing.

A GRASPABLE HANDRAIL, above, is often required by codes. Many builders consider this a nuisance, but Jellema takes the opportunity to create a nice woodworking touch.

CAREFUL ATTENTION TO DETAILS at the bottom corner of a railing can make the difference between a good deck and a great deck, right. This deck is several years old, but the workmanship and the ipé still look like new.

A BALCONY AND ENTRY-PORCH COMBO

A SMALL ENTRY AND AN EVEN SMALLER UPSTAIRS LOOKOUT CAN PRO-
VIDE A BIG VISUAL IMPRESSION IF YOU THINK OUTSIDE THE BOXY LOOK
AND ADD A FEW CURVES. A MIXTURE OF TWO WOOD TONES AND
WHITE TRIM ADDS JUST THE RIGHT AMOUNT OF INTEREST.

DESIGN CONSIDERATIONS

The practical needs here were minimal: no cooking or dining, no large lounge furniture—just a bit of room for sitting and gazing at the water view at the end or beginning of the day. The home was built with an inset entryway that was made for a typical straight-across balcony at the second level. The owners and Jellema decided to add a modest amount of flair.

ENTRY PORCH. With no use areas to plan around, Jellema was free to think of the lower deck simply in terms of aesthetics—though on a pretty small canvas. In keeping with the stately house, he steered clear of ornate decoration. However, he did want to add a bit of fun. The solution is a simple curved shape with straightforward trim.

In practical terms, only one of the two stairs actually leads to a pathway. But having mirrored stairs on either side seems to give the structure wings of a sort.

A railing would have spoiled the view, so the deck needed to be lowered at its front edge. The owner didn't want a step at the door, so the solution was a lowered section, 16 inches wide, wrapping around the front. This front lip is a good width and height for sitting.

BALCONY. The balcony's curved front is the same arc as that on the porch below. The framing is supported in the front by a visible cedar beam and posts, stained to look like the ipé rail posts above. The railing's decorative balusters have a classic look that goes well with brick walls.

MATERIALS. You probably notice that the ipé decking here is unfin-ished. Although most of Clemen's clients prefer finished hardwood decks, the mellow tans and silvers contrast less strongly with the brick walls and the white trim. Unfinished hardwood is a bit easier to main-tain—you just clean it rather than cleaning and applying finish—but it is more susceptible to staining if, say, red wine or dirty oil is spilled on it.

AN ENTRY DECK that welcomes visitors breaks up a brick facade. The white risers and fascia on the front of the deck and the upper-level balcony are made of PVC to match the existing window trim. The steps shown below lead to a path, but those on the other side of the entry lead nowhere and are there to provide design balance.

PLAN VIEW

Upper-Level
Railing

3" Decking Trim

1½" Decking Trim

4x4 Posts

½" Fascia

MATERIALS USED FOR THIS DECK

Framing
(all treated)

6x6 posts
4x4 posts
(for front of lower deck
and for the upper deck)
2x8 ledgers and joists
Doubled 2x8 lower beam
2x12 stair stringers

Decking
and Fascia

5⁄4x6 ipé decking
½ in. PVC fascia board

Railing

4x4 ipé posts
2x4 ipe top and bottom rails
5⁄4x6 ipe cap rail
Metal balusters

INSTALLING A LEDGER ON A BRICK WALL

Your building department will probably have codes for installing and flashing a
ledger on a brick wall. Here's one common method: drill pilot holes through the
ledger for the lag screws. Hold the ledger temporarily in place, and use a masonry bit to make locator holes in the brick wall. Remove the ledger, and drill
holes of the correct size for lag shields. Tap in the shields; reposition the ledger;
and drive the lag screws into the shields.

   To install flashing, use a grinder to cut about 1 inch deep into a line of mortar
above the ledger. Bend a strip of flashing to fit into the cut mortar line and
around the top of the ledger, as shown. Test for fit; remove; and squirt a bead of
exterior caulk into the cut mortar line. Press the flashing into the caulk, and allow
the caulk to dry before you install the joists.

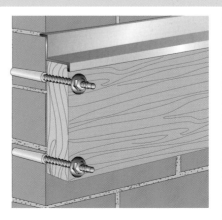

CONSTRUCTION TECHNIQUES

FRAMING FOR A CURVE. Attach the ledger; then build the framing using temporary supports. When framing for a deck with a curved front, first attach the outside joists to the ledger and support them. Then add the beam, using cleats to hold it in position under the joists. Add one or two more temporary supports for the beam. Attach the other joists to the ledger (resting them on the beam) using joist hangers.

Tack a board on top of the joists to keep them the right distance apart. Now mark the top of the joists for the curved front. To do this, you can make a crude compass out of pencil and string: tack the string to the center of the deck section, away from the front, and tie a pencil on the other end. However, if the deck is not long enough, you may not get the curve you want using this method. Another method is to bend a board and hold it on top of the joists. Depending on how tight the curve is, you may use a piece of one-by, a fascia board, a piece of composite decking, or the kerf-cut header joist. (See below.) Have a couple of helpers hold the board in place while you check it for a smooth curve.

Once the joists' tops are marked, use a square to draw lines down each side of the boards. Set your circular saw to mimic the angle of the cut and cut. (The angle will change for each joist.)

FRAMING THE FRONT STEP. Where a deck has a long step, various methods of framing are possible. This is a good method because it makes use of the beam: attach joists to the beam using joist hangers. You may not need to temporarily support them because they are so short. Mark and cut them for a curve that matches the larger deck's curve; you will need to support each joist as you cut it. Add a kerf-cut header joist. Install 4x4 posts as needed.

Build the two side stairs using standard 2x12 stringers. You may simply place them in a gravel bed, or codes may require that they be supported with a concrete slab or with posts set in footings.

THE UPPER DECK. To ensure safety while working, use a couple of sturdy ladders. It's also a good idea to tack a piece of plywood on the joists to provide a working surface. Install the ledger; then build the posts and beam with their tops at the same level as the

ledger's bottom. Install joists; mark for a curve; and cut the joists as you did on the lower deck.

DECKING, FASCIA, AND RAILING. The lower-level decking has a narrow front border. Install the basic decking first, allowing it to run wild. Mark the decking for a curved cut that follows the outside edge of the framing. Cut the decking using a circular saw—or a jigsaw if you are confident of your ability to cut a smooth line. For the front border, rip-cut a piece of decking to 1 inch wide; this will cause it to overhang the ½-inch fascia board by ½ inch. Bend the border into place; drill pilot holes; and drive screws horizontally into the decking.

Here, the upper railing was installed first; then the fascia was fit between the posts. If you are using wood fascia, you may choose to install the fascia first.

White PVC fascia boards are easy to bend, making them an ideal material for curves. One-by cedar would also make this curve, but hardwood fascia would need to be kerf-cut before bending.

Wrap the visible post and beam with decking.

FINE DECKS, INC.

Framing Detail

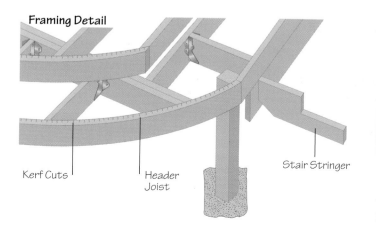

Kerf Cuts   Header Joist   Stair Stringer

KERF CUTS typically extend about halfway through the thickness of a board. The deeper and more closely spaced the cuts, the more the board will bend. As with all outside joists, Jellema typically doubles the headers.

A RESTFUL RETREAT

THIS THREE-LEVEL DECK FORMS A BRIDGE OVER A POND, THEN AMBLES OVER TO A SPA. A PERGOLA OUTFITTED WITH SPEAKERS PROVIDES PARTIAL SHADE AND RESTFUL TUNES FOR THE SOAKERS. COOKING AND DINING AREAS ARE NEARER THE HOUSE. OVER TIME, AS THE LANDSCAPING MATURES, THE SETTING WILL FEEL MORE LIKE A PRIVATE RETREAT WITH NO NEED FOR FENCING.

DESIGN CONSIDERATIONS

FINE DECKS, INC.

To create the owner's ideal outdoor space, Jellema became attuned to their unique vision. He worked closely with a landscaper to achieve a harmonious result.

SOFTNESS AND SECLUSION. The owner had some very general (and ambitious) goals: a space that feels soft rather than harsh and angular; and a true sense of privacy without the use of overt walls. Some of this is achieved by the use of cascading decking tiers, each a different shape, that gently step down to a spa. The variety of angles, as well as the multiple small spaces, cushion the effect of a hard decking surface and make it feel more intimate than the usual deck. The soft beige and brown colors of the composite decking also contribute.

But it is the combination of construction and foliage that will complete the project. Most of the photos here show the deck soon after the vines, bushes, and flowers were planted. That gives a good view of how the deck was constructed, but it does not capture the overall feel that they were trying to achieve. Once the roses and wisteria climb and bloom and the trees and bushes reach maturity, the spa area will be almost completely enclosed. The dining and cooking areas will be more open to the world but will also be more sheltered than they are now.

The owners eat most of their meals on the deck, where they already feel a relaxed sense of nature's presence. Neighbor children enjoy coming over to feed the fish in the pond.

USEFUL SPACES. The three levels may appear random in design, but they are purposefully sized and shaped. The upper level has a bump-out just the right size for a grill and a person or two tending to it. The middle level has room for a dining table. The pathway through the two levels is unobstructed.

The owners decided against built-in planters or benches, prefer-ring the option of moving furniture and pots at will. This gives the deck an open, uncluttered look.

THE SPA DECK. At the lower level, the spa is positioned off to the side, allowing for a sizable lounging area. On one side of the spa is a short wall with a 2×8 ledge at the spa's height. This simple touch allows for people to rest drinks or to sit and dangle their feet in the water.

Overhead is a pergola that by itself offers minimal shade. However, once the wisteria and roses climb over it, the benefits will multiply and provide relief from the sun.

An integrated sound system, operable from the house or from near the spa, uses speakers attached to the top of the pergola at all four corners for a surround-sound experience. Speakers like this are made for outdoor use. Small, low-voltage floodlights point down at the deck and the spa; the lights are not overly bright and can be swiveled to achieve the desired effect.

MULTIPLE LEVELS  seem to flow from the house to the spa at the far end of the deck, right. The goal was to create an un-structured-looking design that is actually quite organized, with each area serving a specific purpose.

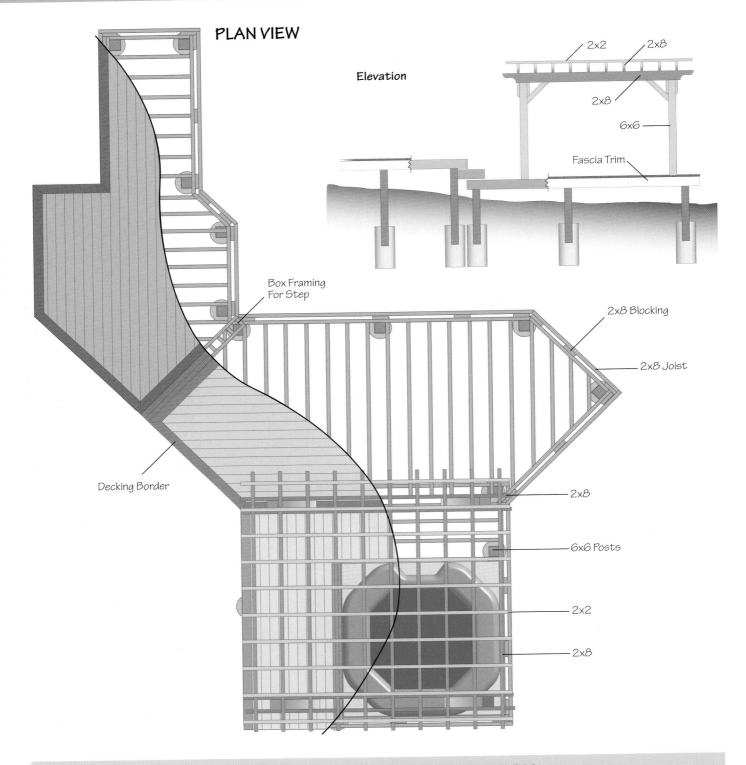

PLAN VIEW

Elevation

2x2

2x8

2x8

6x6

Fascia Trim

Box Framing
For Step

2x8 Blocking

2x8 Joist

Decking Border

2x8

6x6 Posts

2x2

2x8

MATERIALS USED FOR THIS DECK

		Pergola	
Framing (all treated)	6x6 posts 2x8 ledgers, joists, and flush beams 2x4 ledge wall framing		6x6 posts 2x8 beams and rafters 2x2 top pieces
Decking and Fascia	2x6 composite decking, in two colors ½-in. fascia board		

CONSTRUCTION TECHNIQUES

Because it is low to the ground and the individual levels are relatively small, the framing is built with flush beams rather than the more common under-joist beams. In general, it's best to build each framing section with perimeter and interior joists; then add blocking and sister joists to the perimeter—to make all the perimeter joists into flush beams and to provide nailing surfaces for the brown perimeter decking band. Codes will probably require that the joists be attached to the flush beams via joist hangers.

FRAMING THE LEVELS. When the ground is relatively level and the deck is low, you can build the framing for each level individually. Keep in mind that after you add the blocking, the extra joist, and the decking overhang, the finished deck will be significantly larger—it will extend 4½ inches beyond the outside of the first perimeter joist.

Working on the ground or another flat surface, cut the perimeter joists to length and assemble them, checking to make sure the angles are square or at the desired angles as you go. Use a power nailer, or drive screws; hand nailing will shake the boards too much. Use 22½-degree bevel cuts for the 45-degree angles. Once the outside frame is assembled, double-check to see that it is square and has the correct dimensions.

Cut the inside joists, and attach by backnailing through the perimeter joists; make sure all the joist tops are flush. (Later, you may need to add joist hangers.)

THE SPA. A spa (a. k. a. hot tub, whirlpool, or Jacuzzi) must rest on a solid surface; it must be connected to plumbing and electrical service; and

SPAS SHOULD SIT on a concrete pad. The spa manufacturer will have complete installation instructions. Note the hatch that provides access to the plumbing connections.

there must be an access panel for servicing the utilities. Consult with the manufacturer; it is usually best to install a concrete slab and rough in the utilities—and perhaps install the spa, as well—before you build the deck. You are probably best off hiring a spa company to do this for you.

POSTS AND FOOTINGS. Position a framing section where it should go; check again for square; and mark for the postholes. Where possible, place posts at corners so that they can attach to two perimeter joists. Move the framing section, and dig the holes as required by local codes.

REPOSITION THE FRAMING. Working with helpers, raise the frame to the desired height; check for level; and support the frame temporarily.

Cut posts to length, and attach to the framing; the posts will hang down into the holes. Check again for level. Pour concrete, and allow it to cure.

FRAMING THE STEP. Between the middle and the bottom level there is a single step. Frame and temporarily support the middle level; then frame the bottom level. Build a simple framing box for the step, and attach it onto the bottom frame. Raise and temporarily support the bottom level so that the step comes up against the bottom of the middle level.

PERGOLA POSTS. Also dig holes for the pergola posts. These may need to be deeper and have more concrete than the structural posts to keep the pergola firm. Attach the posts to the framing, as well.

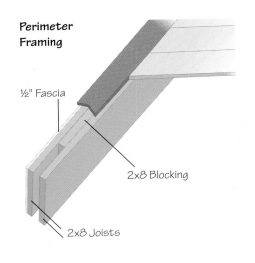

Perimeter Framing

½" Fascia

2x8 Blocking

2x8 Joists

THE PERGOLA serves a few purposes. It provides a vertical design element and partially hides the garage behind it. Once covered with climbing plants, it will provide needed shade for those using the spa.

FLUSH BEAM AND NAILING SURFACE FOR THE DECKING BAND.

When you have a decorative band of decking running around the perimeter, be sure to think through how you will provide the band`and the rest of the decking with a solid nailing surface. Here, the solution is to use blocking and an added joist, to provide in essence a 4½-inch-thick beam. (See the drawing, left.) After allowing for the fascia board and the decking overhang, you will have a good nailing surface.

Cut blocking pieces, about 16 inches long, and attach them at intervals so the gaps between them are no longer than 24 inches. Take care to keep their tops perfectly flush with the tops of the perimeter joists. Then add the outside perimeter pieces, again keeping everything flush so the decking band will rest on a smooth surface.

DECKING.

The decking shown has its own hidden fasteners, which fit into grooves in the sides of the decking. With other types, you may drive screws through the face of the decking.

Install the interior decking pieces first, allowing them to run wild past the point where they will be cut for the band. Use a chalk line to mark for cutting the decking parallel with the perimeter framing and allowing for the border and its overhang. Set a circular saw to cut just deep enough (don't cut deeply into the framing), and perhaps use a straightedge guide when making the cuts.

Cut and fit the decorative band. This will be very visible, so take the time to make precise cuts at the corners.

THE PERGOLA.

Cut the posts to the same height. Cut the 2x8 beam pieces

A WIDE BOARD that tops a 2×4-framed wall enclosed one side of the spa. The ledge comes in handy for setting down drinks or snacks, and serving as a seat near the spa.

to length; then cut decorative ends. Do the same for the 2×8 rafters. Install the beam pieces on each side of the posts, one rafter's width below the top of the posts. Use a nail or two to hold the pieces in place; then drill holes, and attach lag bolts with washers and nuts.

Mark the tops of the beams for regularly spaced rafters. Attach the outside rafters to the sides of the posts. Attach the other rafters by drilling angled holes and driving decking screws. Cut the 2×2 top pieces at a simple decorative angle. Mark the tops of the rafters for even spacing, and attach the top pieces with a single nail or screw at each joint.

THE SPA LEDGE. Next to the spa, build a simple wall by it attaching to one of the pergola posts at one end and to a post at the other end. Make framing out of treated 2×4. Cap the wall with a 2×8 or wider board. Cover the outside of the wall with decking boards, and rip and cut trim pieces to cover the open joints.

NEATLY CUT AND JOINED composite decking can be surprisingly pleasing in appearance, especially when framed by a contrasting border.

A DECK WITH WINGS

THIS FANCIFUL DECK HAS TWO COMFY LIVING SPACES DEFINED WITH NON-SYMMETRICAL SHAPES, WHICH ADD INTEREST AND SEEM TO INCREASE THE SENSE OF LIFE'S POSSIBILITIES. THOUGH IT'S ALL MADE WITH ANGLES, DEEP WOOD TONES MAKE IT FEEL ORGANIC RATHER THAN STRUCTURED.

FINE DECKS, INC.

DESIGN CONSIDERATIONS

A TOUCH OF CHAOS. Decks often aim for a satisfying symmetry; for instance, if a rectangle has a 45-degree angle lopped off on one end, there will often be the same angle of the same size on the other end. Here, however, a bit of gentle havoc is generated simply by increasing the angle on the left-side corner so it is slightly more open than 45 degrees. As a result, the front edge of the right portion is slightly out of line with the angled corner on the left section. The small lack of symmetry makes the deck feel curved even though it isn't.

A DECK AS FLOATING PATIO. The yard was already stunningly land-scaped, with a pool and several types of patio surfaces. Jellema wanted the deck to increase the richness of the materials but not clash with the patio feel that the yard already had. Rather than having four or five steps leading to the patio, Jellema installed a small landing with two steps at the door. Two unobtrusive steps lead from the deck to the patio.

The yard does slope a bit, but the owners didn't want a step down from one deck area to another. So the right side (looking at the photo) was made at nearly ground level, and the left side was allowed to rise a bit more than a foot above grade, giving the surface a floating appearance.

TWO ROOMS. Cooking and dining take place on the patio, so the deck is just for relaxing and getting together with friends. On the left is a squarish area that accommodates a nearly formal living room. On the right is a smaller area, suitable for a couple of people to read or converse. The two rooms are marked off by a decking divider strip; the decking meets the strip at 45-degree angles on each side.

THE DECKING FINISH. The varying shades of decking boards was by design. Repeated applications of sealer (over the more than five years since the deck was built) just naturally highlighted the differences in the boards. The uneven color could be corrected by carefully applying more sealer or a stain to the lighter boards, but the owners like it as is.

LANDING AND RAILING. A 4-foot-deep landing at the door makes it more pleasant to walk out of the house and enter the deck than would a simple set of stairs. It also provides a nice platform for large potted plants that are raised slightly above the decking level.

A SEMI-SECLUDED LIVING AREA, top, occupies one wing of this deck. The other is more open and faces the pool.

AN ENTRY LAND-ING, right, gives prominence to the connection between the house and deck.

CONSTRUCTION TECHNIQUES

PLAN VIEW

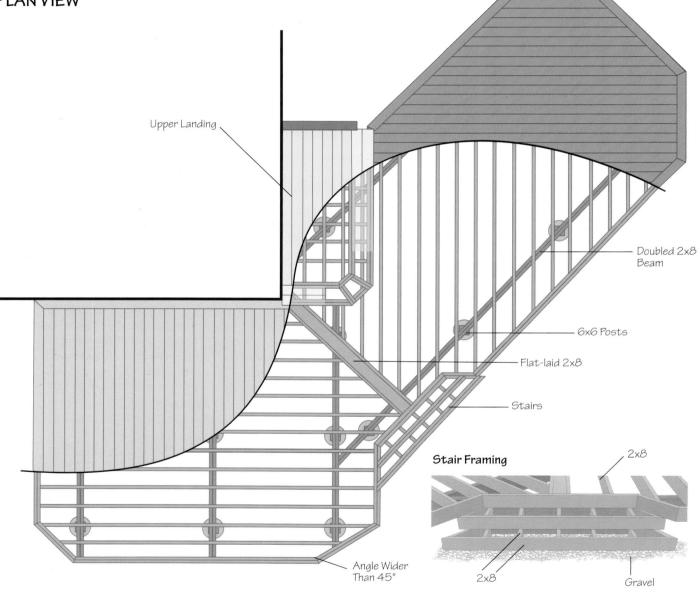

Upper Landing

Doubled 2x8 Beam

6x6 Posts

Flat-laid 2x8

Stairs

Stair Framing

2x8

2x8

Gravel

Angle Wider Than 45°

MATERIALS USED FOR THIS DECK

		Railing	4x4 ipé posts
Framing (all treated)	6x6 posts 2x8 joists and ledgers- Doubled 2x8 beams		2x4 ipé top and bottom rails 1x4 ipé rail cap Metal balusters
Decking and Fascia	1x6 ipé decking		

SEPARATE DECK AREAS by changing the direction of the decking. Here, Jellema divided the two parts of the deck by installing a divider strip and running the decking at a 45-deg. angle to it.

Use high-quality treated lumber rated for ground contact or in-ground use for boards that come near the ground. Frame the main deck first; then build the landing on top of the deck framing.

MAIN DECK FRAMING. Attach the ledger for the main deck. It will be two steps down from the house's door; when figuring the ledger's height, take into account the height of the landing and its step, including the thickness of the decking.

Starting at one end, work with a helper or two to attach the perimeter framing pieces—the outside joists, the headers, and the angled pieces. Temporarily support each piece, checking for level and square as you go. After you have installed several perimeter pieces, go back and recheck; you will likely need to make corrections. Build the perimeter for the left portion first. Check again for square and level. Dig the footing holes. Add the inside joists, spaced every 12 or 16 inches depending on the type of decking and whether or not it will run at an angle to the joists. Jellema then adds sister joists to the outside and header joists for extra strength.

Attach one of the beam pieces, and then the second, using cleats to hold them temporarily in place. (See "Joists and Beams," on page 101.) Cut the posts; hang them from the joists so they go into the footing holes; and pour concrete as required.

LOWER STEPS. To build steps that go low to the ground, the area must be excavated to leave room for the framing. Build framing boxes, with evenly spaced joists for each of the steps. Make the boxes deeper than the steps so that one can rest on top of the other. If possible, attach the first box to the main deck's beam. On this deck, the lower step's framing rests on a bed of gravel; local codes may require other types of support.

Make sure that there will be ample nailing for the decking divider strip and the decking pieces on either side. To provide a wide-enough platform, sandwich a flat-laid 2×6 or 2×8 between joists; make sure all the top surfaces are perfectly flush with each other.

LANDING. The landing and its step can be built on top of the main deck's framing, or it can be added after the decking is laid. There are two basic approaches. For one, you can build a lower framing box (for the step) that extends all the way to the house; then build the upper box on top of that. This method is a bit wasteful of materials. Another option is to build a smaller lower box, extending a few inches under the upper box; then attach a ledger board for the upper level, and have the upper-level framing rest on the lower level only at the front.

DECKING AND FASCIA. Install the decking so that it runs wild past the outside edges of the framing. Where the center strip will go, cut the decking at 45-degree angles, and install it so the boards come within several inches of each other.

Once the main decking is attached, cut it to accommodate the outside border pieces and the divider strip. Use a chalk line to mark for cutting around the perimeter. Lay the center strip in place, and scribe with a pencil for cutting the decking on each side.

PLUGGING IN

Many contractors plug their equipment into an outdoor receptacle, which usually works fine. However, if they overload a circuit (which can easily happen when using saws and compressors), a circuit breaker will trip, meaning that someone has to go to the service panel and reset the breaker. That can be a problem if the owner is not home. To avoid an awkward situation, some contractors, like Jellema, hook their cords directly to an outdoor electrical box, usually the one for the central air conditioner, which is normally a high-amp circuit.

TALL AND NEAT

NEIGHBORS TALK ABOUT HOW THEY ENVY THE OWNERS OF THIS
THREE-LEVEL DECK, WHICH INCLUDES A STAIRWAY CONNECTING UP-
STAIRS TO DOWNSTAIRS. THE VINYL SURFACES STAY IN PRISTINE CONDI-
TION, MAKING FOR A DOLLHOUSE LOOK ON A DECK THAT IS AT THE
SAME TIME EMINENTLY PRACTICAL.

THREE LEVELS not only provide distinct living areas, they—and the connecting stairs—provide a convenient route from the kitchen down to the walk-out basement.

DESIGN CONSIDERATIONS

What looks in the photo to be this house's upstairs is actually the first floor; because of a severe slope, the basement ends up at ground level at the backyard.

THREE LEVELS. Three considerations helped determine the shape of the deck. First, the owners wanted a pleasant dining area near the kitchen, which is off of the upper level, but they didn't need space for a grill near the dining table; like many people, they objected to the smoke. Second, though they had plenty of room in the backyard, they thought that a large raised deck would look out of proportion next to the house. Third, they wanted an easy way to reach the basement level from the kitchen.

The design Jellema came up with is well suited to the house's proportions. It uses a long, 13-step stairway to reach a landing just large enough for an outdoor couch; then it takes three more steps down to a basement-level deck of moderate proportions.

The three deck surfaces are ideal for people who like to entertain only a few friends and who like to have options for reading and relaxing. The lower levels are far enough away from the upper level to gain seclusion when it is desired.

THE ADVANTAGES OF VINYL. For those interested in a pristine-looking deck, vinyl (also called PVC) may be an ideal choice. It has a glossy surface—the railing and fascia are glossier than the decking—that wipes clean easily, and it resists mold and mildew. A simple spraying or sweeping are often all that's needed to restore vinyl to a brand-new appearance.

Many companies make vinyl decking, railing, and fascia, and quality varies greatly. If possible, find an owner with a vinyl deck that is three or more years old and is in a similar position—sitting in bright sunlight or under a shedding tree, for example—and learn how the surfaces have weathered before making your choice.

FINISHING TOUCHES. Jellema's careful attention to detail in every part of the deck results in a very neat appearance. The area below the deck is filled with large gravel for low maintenance. Heavy landscaping fabric under the gravel keeps weeds from popping up.

The structural posts are simply made of pressure-treated lumber, but care was taken to choose the best boards, so they look surprisingly finished and clean.

The manufactured railing system has numerous pieces—post caps, rails, balusters, and trim pieces—that fit together tightly, with virtually no possibility of seams coming apart.

LIKE MOST HIGH DECKS, this one is completely exposed to the sun, so a dining table definitely needs an umbrella. The vinyl decking and railing were chosen because of their resistance to fading in the sun.

PLAN VIEW

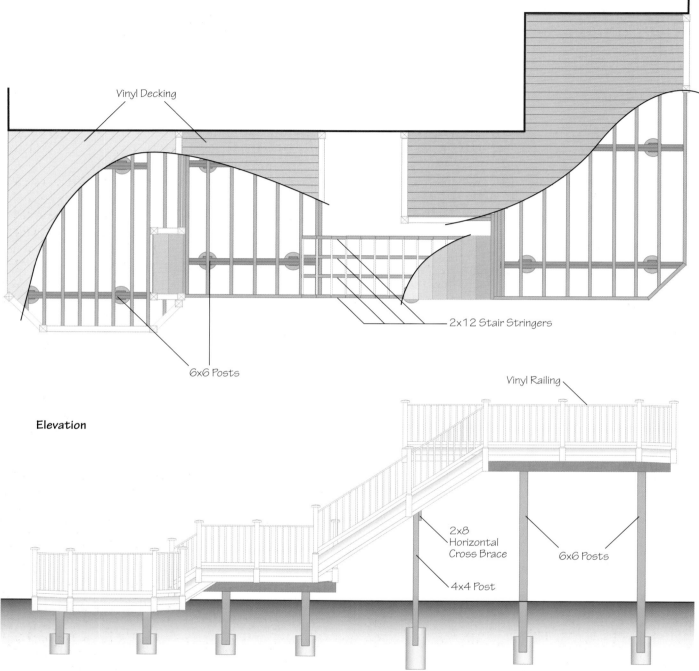

Vinyl Decking

6x6 Posts

2x12 Stair Stringers

Vinyl Railing

Elevation

2x8 Horizontal Cross Brace

6x6 Posts

4x4 Post

MATERIALS USED FOR THIS DECK

Framing (all treated)	6x6 posts 4x4 posts (for middle stair supports) 2x8 ledgers and joists Doubled 2x10 beams 2x12 stair stringers	Decking and Fascia	Vinyl decking Vinyl railing system Vinyl fascia boards
		Railing	All-vinyl manufactured railing system Treated 4x4 posts (to be covered with vinyl sleeves)

CONSTRUCTION TECHNIQUES

Building a raised deck involves some danger and calls for special skills and experience, not to mention good ladders and/or scaffolding, as well as a couple of able helpers.

FRAMING THE DECKS. Install the ledger boards, and add the flashing as required. Now comes the trickiest part—constructing the framing box when you're high in the air. Cut the outside and header joists to length. Working with two helpers, have someone hold each end of a board; you should have temporary support boards ready to use. Have another person check for level and square; then drive screws or nails to attach to the ledger and to fasten to the temporary support. Keep adding perimeter boards this way until you have completed the box. Check again for level and square.

Lay out for joists every 12 or 16 inches, and install them using joist hangers at the ledger and back nailing elsewhere. Cut one beam piece to length, and hang it using a cleat. Add the second beam piece, and laminate the two pieces together with a series of nails or screws.

Hang a plumb bob (or a chalk-line box) from the beams to locate the postholes. Dig the postholes to the required depth. Notch-cut the posts and attach them to the beams so that they hang into the holes. Pour concrete as required.

FRAME THE OTHER DECKS. To locate the height and position of the middle deck, calculate the rise and run of the stairs that connect to the upper deck. Frame for the two other decks in the same way as the upper deck—though they will be easier because they are lower.

Note that with some railing systems, you install 4x4 pressure-treated railing posts (which will be covered later with vinyl sleeves) inside the framing; this must be done before the decking is run. On this deck, however, the posts are installed outside the framing, so the decking can be installed first.

EVEN WHERE IT IS NOT REQUIRED BY CODE, Jellema often installs an extra beam near the house. This way, the deck does not actually rely on the ledger board for support. Most posts connect to the beam using two carriage bolts, but where a beam is spliced, he uses four bolts.

WHEN DECKING AROUND AN OBSTRUCTION, use fascia board to trim the inside edges.

DECKING. Like many vinyl decking products, this one comes with its own hidden-fastener system. In a typical system, you may need to drive a screw through the face of one side on the first board. Slip fasteners into the decking's groove on the other side, and drive screws through the fasteners into joists. Slide the next decking piece into place so that the fasteners slip into its groove, and repeat the operation.

Here, the decking is cut flush to the edge of the framing; the fascia board will be installed with its top flush with the decking surface. This method adds a nice thin white border to the deck surface, but it calls for excellent carpentry skills because the joints are visible. An easier method is to run the decking 1½ inches past the framing, and install the fascia tucked under the decking.

THE STAIRS. Install a secure hanger board below the upper level's joist to gain a surface to which you can attach the stringers. After you have calcu-lated the individual rise and run, cut a notched stringer. Hold it in place to be sure it fits and that all the rises and runs are the same dimensions. Use the first stringer as a template for marking and cutting the others. Here, two stringers and a carriage would have passed code, but Jellema uses a second carriage for a strong stairway.

A set of 4x4 posts and a cross-brace are needed to support the center of a long stairway like this. Use a plumb bob (or a chalk-line box) to locate the postholes. Dig the holes; hang the posts; and pour concrete as you did for the 6x6 posts. Attach a horizontal brace, running from post to post, to support the interior stringers.

THE RAILING SYSTEM. A vinyl railing system is basically a kit with post sleeves, top and bottom rails, rail connectors, balusters, post caps, and various trim pieces. Following the manufacturer's instructions, first install 4x4 pressure-treated rail posts no more than 6 feet apart. Cut post sleeves to fit, and slip them over the posts. Add the rails and balusters; then finish with the trim pieces.

LOW-MAINTENANCE VINYL DECKS will look good for years with minimal care on your part. This system includes a hidden-fastener attachment system.

FINE DECKS, INC.

THIS STAIRWAY USES TWO NOTCHED STRINGERS and two carriages, right. Extra blocking is added, as well as a pair of 4x4 posts and a horizontal cross brace, to stiffen the stringers.

VINYL RAILING SYSTEMS, below, come in kits that usually contain all of the exterior parts necessary for installation. For the posts, attach pressure-treated lumber to the framing, and then cover them with the vinyl sleeve.

MAKING THE MOST OF A SMALL SPACE

THIS WOOD-AND-COMPOSITE DECK HAS A SURPRISINGLY NATURAL
FEEL AND FOLLOWS THE CONTOURS OF THE SMALL SITE. A BENCH
TAKES THE PLACE OF A RAILING IN THE BACK.

BY MOVING THE DECK AWAY FROM THE HOUSE, the basement was not deprived of natural light. Note the window wells between the shrubs. A bench that runs the full length of the deck provides extra seating and does not block the view of those inside the house looking out at the deck.

FINE DECKS, INC.

DESIGN CONSIDERATIONS

The backyard is small, with an existing patio and a stone walkway that the owners wanted to keep. To tighten the space even more, they wanted to keep the deck away from two basement window wells in order to maintain the minimal sunlight in the basement. So the deck nearly follows the contours of the stone path and is about 5 feet away from the wall with the window wells.

The materials of choice are tan composite decking and tropical hardwood for the fascia and railing—a great-looking combination. The hardwood would be difficult to bend for fascia and the railing, so it was decided to follow the path using a half-octagon rather than a curve.

For the back of the deck, the building inspector cut Jellema some slack and allowed him to build a bench, even though a railing is officially required when a deck is higher than 2 feet.

CONSTRUCTION TECHNIQUES

Attach a ledger to the area near the house's door. Build the framing, supported temporarily as you work. Install the decking. Jellema doubles up all the outside joists for added strength and so that the railing and the bench will not wobble.

Calculate the rises and runs, and cut and install stair stringers on either side. Attach the stair treads and the ipé risers.

Attach the railing posts and the posts for the back of the bench, which should be about 16 inches above the decking. Attach the bottom and top rails to the posts, and attach the balusters to the rails. Add the top cap.

For the bench, cut the front posts so that they are the same height as the back posts when resting on the decking. Build a simple 2x4 frame to run around the posts, and add short 2x4 treated joists to run crosswise on the inside of the frame. Attach the decking to form the bench.

MATERIALS USED FOR THIS DECK

Framing (all treated)	6x6 posts 2x8 ledger and joists Doubled 2x10 beams 2x12 stair stringers
Decking and Fascia	⁵⁄₄x6 composite decking 1x6 ipé fascia and stair risers
Railing	4x4 ipé posts 2x4 ipé top and bottom rails ⁵⁄₄x6 ipé cap rail
Bench	4x4 ipé posts 2x4 ipé and treated lumber for framing, composite decking for seat

PLAN VIEW

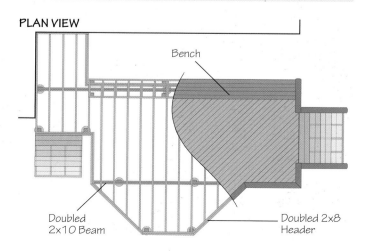

Bench

Doubled 2x10 Beam

Doubled 2x8 Header

FINISHING TOUCHES

LIKE MANY DECK BUILDERS, JELLEMA IS ADEPT AT DESIGNING AND
BUILDING AMENITIES THAT MAKE A DECK FEEL MORE LIKE HOME.
HERE ARE A FEW SAMPLES.

PLANTER/BENCH

The unit shown left, with two planters and three benches, creates a cozy gathering place, just the right size to surround a firepit. All the visible surfaces are ipé. You could use redwood, cedar, treated lumber, or composite instead, but the benches will need more supports to keep from sagging. The planters can be filled directly with soil, or they can be used as containers for flowerpots.

You can build this after the deck is completed; there's no need to anchor it to the deck's framing. Use 2x6s for the seat pieces; treated 2x4s for the framing, and 1x6 tropical hardwood for all the other pieces. If you are not using a tropical hardwood, use treated lumber for all the parts that will touch soil or that will support flowerpots.

THE PLANTERS. Build simple planter frames out of 2x4s. At some of the joints, you will need to angle-drive screws or nails. The cleats will support the planter bottom pieces; position them according to how deep you want the soil to be (or how tall the flowerpots will be).

Planter Bench

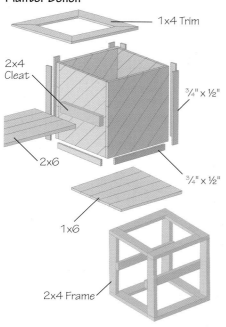

- 1x4 Trim
- 2x4 Cleat
- 3/4" x 1/2"
- 2x6
- 3/4" x 1/2"
- 1x6
- 2x4 Frame

Using a power miter saw, cut hardwood pieces at 45-degree angles to fit over the faces of the frame. Attach them with nails or screws driven near the ends so that their heads will be covered with the trim. Rip-cut 1x6 pieces in half to make the trim. Cut them to length, and install at the corners. Finish by miter-cutting and fastening 1x4 top trim pieces.

THE BENCHES. The bench seat is made of four 2x4s with ¼-inch gaps between them. To support the benches at the planters, attach 2x4 cleats, as long as the seat is wide, to the sides of the planters. Position the cleats 1½ inches below the desired height of the seat (typically, 17 inches). To make a bench support that does not attach to the planter, cut a hardwood 2x4 to the width of the seat. Cut two 4x4s to the height of the seat minus 3 inches, and attach the 2x4 to the top of the 4x4s. Position the planters where you want them to go. Place the 2x6 seat pieces on the cleats and the seat supports. Attach the seat pieces. Add small trim pieces to the bottoms of the 4x4s.

DECK DOORS

The area under a deck may be left open, but often it looks best to cover it with some sort of skirt. If you do that, make sure there will be adequate ventilation. In humid climates, sealing off the underside of

FOR UNDER-DECK VENTILATION install framed lattice panels, as shown here. The frames are made of rot-resistant ipé.

FOR INSTANT STORAGE, close off the underside of the deck and install a door.

a deck can lead to mildew and mold. Also, provide a way to get to the area.

For occasional access to a lattice-skirted deck, make a simple frame out of lattice and trim boards. Below, ipé is used; it is impervious to rot and so can rest in soil. Attach the frame with screws, and unscrew them to gain access.

If you want to get in and out fairly often, go ahead and build a door, above. Frame the area around the door so that the hinge and latch can attach to something solid. Make the door out of the same material as the skirting; here, Jellema matches the angled pattern as well. Make a simple door frame out of 2x4s, and attach the finish material. The door should be about ⅛ inch narrower than the opening so it can open and close easily. Position the door in the opening, and attach the hinges. Add the latch, and fill in the perimeter with trim pieces.

FINE DECKS, INC.

DECK BUILDERS INC.

Kim Katwijk
Deck Builders Inc.
Olympia, Washington
(360) 709-9225
www.artistryindecks.com

DECK BUILDERS INC.

Kim Katwijk (he says it's OK to pronounce it "Cat-wick"), of Deck Builders, Inc. located in Olympia, Washington, prides himself on designing decks with subtle or stunning design twists that make them feel like special places. He also takes extraordinary steps to ensure against wood rot—a persistent problem in the moisture-laden Northwest. The majority of his clients have houses on fairly secluded wooded lots, often overlooking a lake or a portion of Puget Sound. He has been building decks for over 20 years, and splits his time between designing decks, managing two or three crews, and participating in the construction.

KIM KATWIJK designs decks that are divided into separate activity areas, above.

FOR A DIFFERENT LOOK, Katwijk has developed a couple of different railing systems, below and opposite. They do not block the views.

CONCRETE PAVERS are sometimes used by Katwijk, above. The weight requires the use of four-by joists.

TRAFFIC LANES are important elements in Katwijk's designs. Note how the path from the sliders to the yard, below, avoids the built-in seating area.

DESIGNS WITH A DIFFERENCE

Katwijk says his clients typically want a deck that is different but not gaudy. So his designs feature lines that are clean but often with a slightly different angle or a gentle curve. Much of his decking is installed with a hidden-fastener system of his own devising, so there is no grid of fastener heads on the deck. (See page 176.)

To keep the look clean, Katwijk minimizes the use of vertical elements. For example, most of his railings have a smooth, continuous cap rail, rather than having the line interrupted by posts that protrude above the railing. His railings often feature balusters made of rods or cables so thin as to be barely noticeable. Tempered-glass panels are also often used. These types of railings do not hinder the waterfront views that so many of his customers have.

Katwijk often installs decking at an "off angle" to the house. That is, he uses an angle other than 90 degrees or 45 degrees. Though it may not be immediately noticeable, this gives the deck space an organic rather than geometric feel.

In the Northwest, people tend to prefer muted colors that blend with the surroundings rather than calling attention to themselves. When using composite materials, the choices are usually brown or gray; when using wood, stains tend to be mellow rather than bright.

FUNCTION AND COMFORT

A deck must be amply sized for all its activities, with no crowded spaces. Like most good deck builders, Katwijk makes sure that there will be ample room for dining, cooking, and lounging, as well as pathways between the areas.

His curved-back bench design creates seating that is molded to the

contours of the human body. (See page 146.) And he typically positions a spa (a. k. a. hot tub) with its rim 18 to 24 inches or so above the decking surface, which makes it easier to enter and exit than a spa that is at deck level. He then builds seating—at the rim level—around part of the spa so people can easily sit with their feet dangling in the water.

the rot problem that he has spent a good deal of time researching it. Whenever he dismantles an old, rotted deck (something that he often has occasion to do), he examines the boards to see which ones rotted, where they rotted, and why they rotted. Using the knowledge gained, he designs decks that will not repeat those mistakes.

PREVENTING WOOD ROT

The Pacific Northwest is sometimes called "the fungus capital of the U.S.," so Katwijk carefully chooses materials and uses construction methods with an eye toward preventing rot. Even if your area is not as damp as his, consult with your building inspector and your builder to make sure your deck will not suffer rot in a few years.

Katwijk is so devoted to solving

BECAUSE OF THE CLIMATE in the Pacific Northwest, Katwijk selects materials and building techniques that resist moisture, such as the composite deck, above. The screen is made of cedar.

NEARLY INVISIBLE RAILINGS, right, are one of Katwijk's specialities. The goal is not to obstruct the view from the deck. Before building, check to be sure such systems meet code requirements in your area.

DEALING WITH MOSS AND FUNGUS

IN VERY DAMP ENVIRONS, even composite decking and railing materials can be attacked by moss, lichen, or fungus. In Katwijk's area, many boards get a green coating every year. The moss seen here is best dealt with in the fall when the weather is relatively dry. Katwijk recommends mixing a solution of very hot water and a laundry soap that contains bicarbonate. Work when it is shady, so it will not evaporate quickly. Scrub it in with a brush; wait 15 minutes; then rinse thoroughly.

ON MANY OF KATWIJK'S DECKS, vertical elements are kept to a minimum. For example, the deck railing above features a smooth top rail rather than posts that rise above the rail.

Building inspectors and local building departments aim to have specific code requirements that ensure long-lasting decks. And following those codes will often go a long way toward making a deck more durable. However, some local codes are not stringent enough; Katwijk finds that in his area many decks that passed inspection ended up rotten in a few years. Also, there are some things that an inspector cannot see. For instance, the bottom of deck posts and other cut ends of framing lumber will not be visible during an inspection; the builder might just cut the boards and install them, or he might apply sealant to all the cuts. That's why it's important to hire a builder who really cares about building a long-lasting deck and is willing to go beyond code requirements when necessary.

In general, Katwijk prevents rot by allowing wood lumber pieces to air out after a rain. That is, he avoids situations where moisture can collect and sit for long periods. For example, his ledger boards are installed using a hold-off method, which keeps them about an inch away from the house, and decking is also kept away from the house. That way, debris can fall down through the opening and water can flow away—and the deck can air dry quickly. (For these and other specific techniques, see "Katwijk's Techniques," on page 140.)

MATERIALS

Synthetic (composite or vinyl) decking and railing products are very popular among Katwijk's clients for obvious reasons—they don't rot, and they clean easily. They are available in colors that go well with painted siding.

Tropical hardwoods can do well, as long as they are kept well sealed. Hardwood that is allowed to go gray will not rot, but it can easily collect moss and mildew.

Cedar comes in a variety of grades, and Katwijk chooses his carefully. Inexpensive cedar is largely light-colored sapwood, which does not resist rot. Higher-priced cedar that is all dark heartwood does resist rot.

Southern yellow pine is not available in his area—or in many western areas. His lumber suppliers generally carry only hem-fir, which, unfortunately, does not readily accept the pressure-treating liquid. So Katwijk is careful to seal all cut ends.

EXTRA SUPPORT is required when adding a spa. Opposite, the spa is installed below the decking.

KATWIJK'S TECHNIQUES

■ Because the climate is damp and the lumber is not highly rot-resistant, Katwijk does not sink posts into the ground, as do some other builders in this book. He uses an "aboveground post," meaning that the bottom of the post is raised above grade; it rests on a metal post anchor, which is attached to the footing so that it can dry out.

■ Katwijk's method for pouring footings is simple: dig a hole; pour in dry concrete mix; add a preformed concrete pier; and pour some more dry mix around the pier. The ground is so damp that the concrete will have formed and hardened by morning. This method works well and is up to code in his neck of the woods, where the frost line is only 12 inches, but it may not fly with your inspector.

■ When attaching a ledger, Katwijk usually does not cut out a section of siding, which he feels unnecessarily exposes the house's sheathing and framing. Instead, his ledger boards are attached using a hold-off method, which keeps the ledger about an inch away from the house's siding. He has had this ledger tested and approved by engineers at Washington State University. (See age 157 for this method, and page 151 for the method

HIDDEN FASTENERS (See page 176.)

he recommends if codes demand that you cut out the siding and use flashing.)

■ He almost never doubles (or "sisters") framing members— that is, he never attaches boards side by side, which would create a seam where water could infiltrate. Where most builders use doubled two-bys to make a beam, Katwijk uses a solid four-by. When he must double up members—for example, at a curved header—he covers the top of the boards with torch-down roofing membrane to keep moisture from seeping between the boards.

■ Whenever he cuts a treated board, he soaks the cut end in a sealer/preservative. (Not sealing cut ends may void the manufacturer's warranty.)

■ Katwijk is a master at bending composite decking boards to create complex patterns. This is time consuming, but makes for one-of-a-kind decking surfaces.

■ The bottom of a stair stringer is particularly susceptible to water infiltration and rot. Katwijk always rests his stringers on a concrete slab.

■ Katwijk usually installs his joists at 12-inch intervals, even if 16 inches would meet code. He feels that the firmness gained is well worth the extra materials cost.

■ Unlike the three other builders in this book, Katwijk does not build temporarily supported joist framing first, and then add the beams and posts. Instead, he builds largely from the ground up, starting with the footings, then adding ledger, posts, and beams. Then he builds the joist framing.

■ In keeping with the aim of allowing deck elements to dry out, Katwijk installs decking with ⅜-inch gaps between the boards—as opposed to the usual ⅛ inch. Decking is also kept well away from the house. Most debris from trees can easily slip through these wide gaps, making it easy to keep the deck clean and reducing the number of moisture collection points.

■ He has designed his own rod railing system, using modified composition railing parts and thin rods. This maximizes the view through the railing. (See page 177.)

■ Katwijk also has devised his own hidden-fastener system, using anodized washers and screws. (See page 176.)

FOUR-BY BEAMS

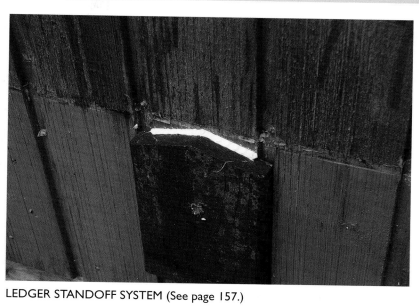

LEDGER STANDOFF SYSTEM (See page 157.)

CURVED DECKING

A BIG DECK WITH A BIG VIEW

THIS DECK MAXIMIZES LAKE VIEWS AND PROVIDES PLENTY OF SPACE AND SEATING OPPORTUNITIES FOR A LARGE GATHERING. RUSTIC POSTS SUPPORT A COMPOSITE DECK WITH GLASS-AND-METAL RAILINGS.

DECK BUILDERS INC.

DESIGN CONSIDERATIONS

Contrary to what many people believe about the "rainy" Northwest, the owners of this deck are able to eat and lounge outdoors most days from May through October. They wanted a comfortable space to relax and enjoy the lake view. They also wanted an area where they could entertain large groups.

The deck is perfectly symmetrical, with a bench and staircase in the middle. Symmetry is often a good choice on a very large deck, which can feel a bit confusing if allowed to ramble all over the place.

THE UPPER DECK. From the house, you step onto a very large upper deck—68 × 12 feet. Here there is more than enough room for dining and cooking areas. The owners liked having an "open" floor plan, which allows them to rearrange furniture as needed.

The house's eave overhangs all along the deck, extending about 4 feet. Because rainfalls in the Northwest are usually light and winds are usually calm, this makes it possible for people to stay pretty dry during rainfalls while they sit on chairs near the house. Because the deck is so long, a good deal of sheltered area is available.

LOWER LEVEL. The design has at its center a circle that is partly formed by a curved section in front of the deck and partly by a wraparound bench at the circle's back. On each side of the circle is a bumped-out "lookout" area, where people can lean against the railing and contemplate the scenery.

Inside the circle is enough room

for a large dining table with chairs. Additional guests can sit on the bench, and there is still room for a comfortable pathway. The bench faces the outward view.

BENCH, STAIRWAY, AND RAILING. The bench features a curved back that makes it more comfortable than the average bench. For additional comfort, seat cushions are added.

The owners considered installing a large, cascading stairway, but they felt that the deck itself is already large enough. The stairs are 4 feet wide—wider than average, and in keeping with the dimensions of the deck; narrower stairs would look skinny. The house has easy access to the garage and garbage area elsewhere, so no side stairs are needed.

The railing is powder-coated metal posts and rails, with tempered glass panels instead of balusters. This costs a bit more than a standard railing but offers the most visibility.

MATERIALS. The composite decking, along with the custom burgundy color of the railing, gives a redwood feel to the deck, but with all the convenience of a synthetic surface. The posts are Douglas fir poles, lightly sealed so they turn a rustic gray.

A LITTLE BUMP OUT on each side of the lower portion of the deck creates a small lookout area that is used for admiring the scenery.

CONSTRUCTION TECHNIQUES

This is a large and fairly complicated structure; tackle a project like this only if you are skilled and have some able helpers.

LAYOUT AND FOOTINGS. When building from the ground up, as Katwijk does, it is very important to get the layout for the footings exactly right—especially the footings that will support the flush beams at the sides. When laying out, measure out from the house, and use triangulation methods to ensure that the footings are square to each other and to the house.

Keep in mind that the perimeter posts will support flush beams (at the same height as the joists) and the other posts will support under-beams (which the joists will rest on).

Dig holes as required by codes, and insert 10-inch concrete tube forms into the holes. Use braces to hold the forms several inches above grade and correctly positioned. Double-check the tubes for correct placement. Pour concrete, and when you reach the top, insert a code-approved post anchor into the concrete. The anchor Katwijk uses here inserts into a slot cut in the bottom of the post.

Install a ledger against the house. (For Katwijk's preferred method, see page 157.)

PLAN VIEW

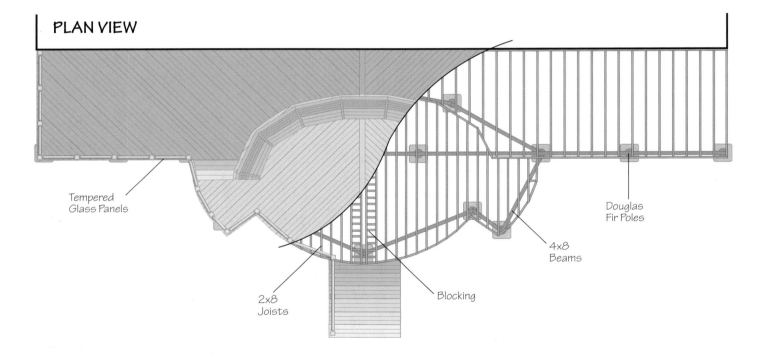

Tempered Glass Panels

Douglas Fir Poles

4x8 Beams

2x8 Joists

Blocking

MATERIALS USED FOR THIS DECK

Framing (all treated)	Rough Douglas fir poles for posts 4x8 beams 2x8 ledgers and joists 2x12 stair stringers	Railing (custom fabricated)	Powder-coated metal posts, rails, and connectors Tempered glass panels
Decking and Fascia	⁵⁄₄x6 composite decking Decking or facia board for fascia	Bench (alternate version)	Treated 4x10 for vertical supports Treated 2x4 for framing Treated 4x4 post Composite decking

DOUGLAS FIR POLES support this and some other of Katwijk's decks. The poles sit atop concrete piers. The bolts shown attach the pole to a post anchor.

CUTTING AND INSTALLING POLES.
Use a transit, a water level, a line level, or a carpenter's level atop a long board; measure to determine the height of each post. The beams will be set in slots in the posts, so the posts are cut to reach within 1–2 inches of the beam's top. The perimeter posts will reach to the top of the joist level; the other posts reach to underneath the joists.

The best tool for working with poles (or logs) is a small chain saw with a 12-inch blade. Use it carefully, always taking care to cut away from your body; position yourself so that if you slip the saw will not come near you. Practice on scrap pieces until you feel comfortable using it.

Cut the poles to height; take into account how much higher the beam will be than the top of the post, as well as the thickness of the roofing materials.

At the bottom of the pole, make a plunge cut or other type of cut, as needed to create a slot into which the concrete anchor will fit. Apply liquid sealer to the cut end. Use a knife to cut a round piece of EPDM or other torch-down roofing material, and use a propane torch to seal it against the cut end. Slip the pole onto the anchor, and check for plumb. Drill holes, and drive bolts to firmly attach the post to the anchor. Use 2x4 braces and stakes to temporarily hold the posts in position as you work on the top of the post.

Use the chain saw to cut a slot for the beam. Make sure that the bottom of the slot is the correct height to support the beam. Mark both sides of the pole for the cut. Have a helper guide you so that you cut both lines correctly. Check the slot for plumb and correct size. Also cut both sides of the slot at an angle so water will run down.

Test-fit the beam, and make sure it is at the correct height; you may need to adjust the notches or insert shims. Once you are sure it will fit, remove it, and apply liquid sealer to the cut portions. Set the beam in place. Finish with strips of water-proofing membrane. Cut sections of torch-down roofing, and use a torch to seal the top of the beam, as well as the top of the posts.

A SMALL CHAIN SAW, above, helps make short work of notching the support posts to accept a beam. Katwijk uses solid four-by beams rather than two laminated two-by beams.

TO COMBAT MOISTURE PENETRATION, Katwijk tops support posts and beams with a torch-down roofing material, right.

ANGLED DECKING adds a distinctive design touch. Install blocking between joists to ensure adequate nailing surfaces.

JOISTS. Once the beams are in place, cut and install the joists. Use joist hangers at the ledger and where the joists join to the flush beams.

At the curve, use a pencil-and-tape-measure compass to mark the tops of the joists, and cut. Cut blocking pieces to fit between the joists; each cut will be at a different angle, so take your time to get these joints tight.

Where the decking will have a center strip, with angled decking on each side, install a series of blocking pieces every 12 inches or so. This will provide ample nailing surface to support the center strip and the decking boards on each side.

DECKING, FASCIA, STAIRS. Install a center strip on the lower and the upper deck; then run the decking out at angles from the strips. Allow the decking to run wild past the joists; then mark with a chalk line; and cut so it overhangs the joists by 2 inches or so. Add the fascia by tucking it under the decking.

For the stairs, cut and install stringers. Add risers and treads.

THE BENCH. The bench will be heavy enough that it can be attached with angle-driven screws or small angle brackets to the top of the deck.

Katwijk has a source for massive 4x16s for the vertical supports; in the drawing below, we show building with more-common 4x10s, plus a 4x4 front post. For each of the seat supports, cut the vertical support to the dimensions shown. Cut 4x4 posts to the height of the seat minus the thickness of the seat pieces. Position all of the supports in place, and cut 2x4s to make a frame that wraps around them. Add 2x4 joists between the vertical supports so that the seat pieces will be supported every 16 inches. Cut and install decking pieces to cover the seat, then the back and the top.

RAILING. Once the deck is completed, have a railing company come out and measure for a custom-fit railing. The posts need to be attached with screws driven into the beams or other solid framing members.

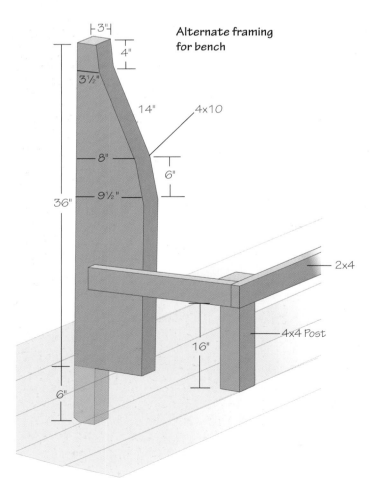

Alternate framing for bench

3"
4"
3½"
14"
4x10
8"
6"
9½"
36"
2x4
4x4 Post
16"
6"

A CURVED BACK on the built-in bench, above, makes for comfortable seating. A framing option is shown at left.

THE POWDER-COATED POSTS and rails, opposite, are designed to withstand the climate with limited maintenance. The posts are attached to the flush beam.

STYLISH ENTRY

THIS SMALL, CURVACEOUS DECK PACKS A BIG VISUAL PUNCH AND
TURNS A SIMPLE OFFICE ENTRYWAY INTO A PLACE TO REMEMBER.

A SMALL ENTRY DECK gets a style boost thanks to an inlaid tile medallion and a curved design. The use of ipé as a decking material also contributes to the success of this deck.

DECK BUILDERS INC.

DESIGN CONSIDERATIONS

The owners of a landscaping company wanted to add some pizzazz to their office entry. Katwijk supplied them with a deck that is so stunning it has become one of his signature creations.

There are few practical considerations here— no outdoor rooms, just a good-looking platform and set of stairs. The nearly circular deck is 12 feet in diameter. A set of four decking tiles, made of natural stone with a fiberglass backing, are set in a diamond pattern in the middle. The decking is divided into three sections by two curved lines that continue onto the set of four stairs.

The stairs themselves open up as they descend, ending on a stone patio. The risers (the vertical spaces between the treads) are kept open rather than being covered with riser boards, which puts the stair framing somewhat on display.

The decking is ipé, an expensive tropical hardwood that gains deeper color as more sealer is applied over the years. The variation in color from board to board enhances the natural beauty. A metal railing is tinted dark brown with black mottles. Its lightly decorative posts add just the right touch of ornamentation.

THERE ARE A LOT OF DETAILS built into this small deck area. The most obvious is the tile medallion, which requires special framing to hold the tiles in place. The curved lines shown here run from the door to the stairs. The railing and stairs flare outward, completing the entire design.

FRAMING PLAN VIEW

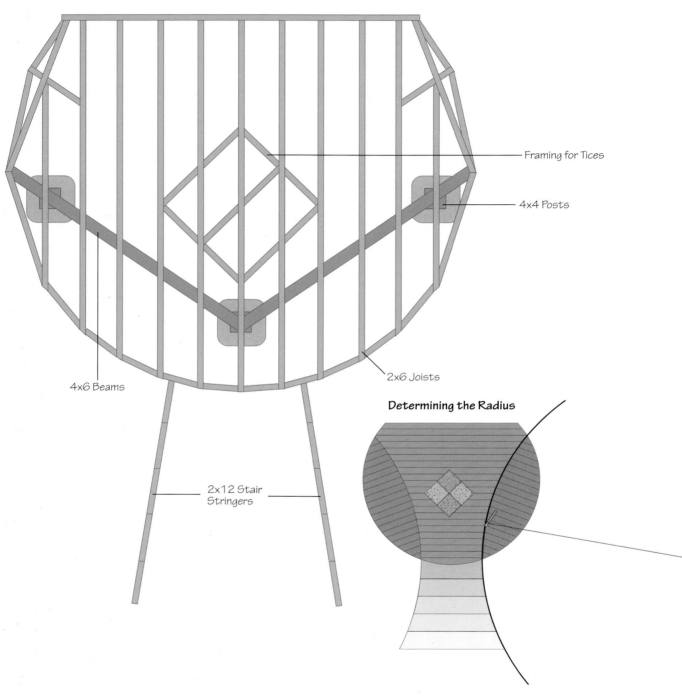

Framing for Tices

4x4 Posts

2x6 Joists

4x6 Beams

2x12 Stair Stringers

Determining the Radius

MATERIALS USED FOR THIS DECK

Framing (all treated)	4x4 posts 4x6 beams 2x6 ledger and joists 2x12 stair stringers	Decking and Fascia	⁵⁄₄x6 ipé decking ³⁄₈" x 6" cedar benderboard for fascia"
		Railing	Custom-fabricated metal railing

CONSTRUCTION TECHNIQUES

This deck has a good number of fine details requiring excellent carpentry skills and careful attention to detail. Many pieces need to be cut at individual angles, so building is time consuming. Here we give instructions for Katwijk's method, which starts with the footings, posts, and beams, and then builds on top of the beam. If you will have in-ground posts, you may choose to start by framing temporarily supported joists, and hang the beams and posts from the joists, as the other deck builders in this book do.

FOOTINGS, LEDGER, POSTS.

Measure and lay out for three footing holes; the posts will support two beams. Position the footings about a foot in from the perimeter of the deck framing. Pour the concrete as required by local codes. (See page 165

for Katwijk's method.) If you are not using precast piers with built-in post anchors, insert post anchors into the wet concrete. Allow the concrete to cure.

Attach the ledger as required. Use spacers to hold the ledger away from the house and allow water to flow behind, or install flashing to keep water from the ledger and the house. Draw layout lines for the joists, and drive screws or bolts to secure the ledger to the house.

Use a transit or other type of level to measure up from each post anchor, and cut a post that is a beam's width below the bottom of the joists, which are at the same level as the ledger. Apply sealer to the cut ends of the posts; slip them into the post anchor; check for plumb; and drive screws or nails to fasten the posts securely to the anchors.

BEAMS. The beams attach to the top of the posts via post caps. Allow the beams to run wild past where the framing will be; you will cut it to length later. At the front post, cut the beams at an angle so that they fit snugly together and both rest securely on top of the post. You will need to use two post caps, and cut them with tin snips to modify them for supporting both beams at this post.

BASIC JOISTS. Build the basic joist framing; then add the complicated-looking angled pieces to support each side of the curve-cut decking. Attach joists to the ledger using joist hangers. Allow them to run wild to be cut to length later. Check that the joists are square to the ledger and are evenly spaced, and attach them to the beams using ties or angle-driven fasteners.

Attaching the Ledger

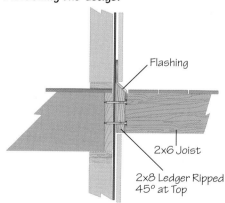

Flashing

2x6 Joist

2x8 Ledger Ripped 45° at Top

FOR MOST OF HIS DECKS, Katwijk uses standoffs to keep the ledger away from the house. Another method, used on this deck, is more like the flashed ledgers used by the other builders in this book. The major difference: Katwijk makes the ledger out of a board that is wider than the joists, and he bevel-cuts the top edge of the ledger so water cannot collect on top of it.

EXTRA FRAMING PIECES are needed for the unusual design of this deck. Note how the angled beams meet at the front post.

FOR THIS COMPLICATED DESIGN, Katwijk used a compass to scribe the radius on the decking boards. The inlaid tiles should be installed at a 45-deg. angle.

Tack a nail at a point in the center of what will be the 12-foot-diameter circle. Because the circle is cut off where it meets the house, this point will be about 42 inches from the house. If the center point does not fall on a joist, tack a board on top of the joists and tack a nail on the board. Hook a tape measure to the nail, and measure out from the nail for a radius of 6 feet all around. The radius should fall at the ends of the ledger. If needed, make adjustments to the center point, or change the radius dimension slightly. Hold a pencil against the tape measure, and mark the tops of the joists for cutting.

Note that the front end of the circle, where the circle will be, will be framed straight across. Mark and cut these joists accordingly.

Each joist will be cut at a different angle. Use a small square to mark each side of each joist. Katwijk cuts these pieces using a small chain saw. Work carefully, always making sure your arms and legs are not in a position to be accidentally cut if the saw should slip. Practice on scrap pieces. You can make these cuts using a circular saw, reciprocating saw, or handsaw, but the work will be very slow, and it will be difficult to make straight cuts on the very steep angles.

Once all the joists are ready, cut blocking pieces to fit between them.

Again, each will need to be cut at a different bevel; take your time to make all the pieces fit snugly. Attach the blocking pieces with power-driven nails.

CUSTOM FRAMING PIECES. Once you have a basic circle, you will need to add short pieces, using blocking, to finish the circle near the ledger on each side.

Mark the top of the joists for where the two curved decking sections will meet. Temporarily fasten a board at the same height as the deck, and tack a nail 13½ feet away from the curved line, as shown in the illustration on page 150. Using a tape-measure-and-pencil compass, mark the tops of the joists for the position of the curved decking lines. (You can see this compass in the photo above.)

Using a circular saw when possible and a reciprocating saw or small chain saw where a shallow angle is needed, cut framing pieces to fit on either side of the curved line. This may take a day or two.

Also install framing pieces to support the tiles in the center of the deck. The tiles used here call for fiberglass support strips, as shown in the photo on page 151.

DECKING. Install the tiles, making sure they are at a perfect 45-degree

angle to the house. Cut decking pieces at a 45-degree angle, and position several on the deck. Use a tape-and-pencil compass to mark the curve, and cut with a jigsaw or a circular saw. You will need a sharp blade to cut through the hardwood.

When cutting decking boards on the other side of the curve, place them on top of the already-cut boards, and mark with the compass. Cut and install. Let the other end of these pieces run wild, and use a compass positioned as you did for cutting the joists to mark for the outside cut.

For fascia, use clear, vertical-grain ⅜-inch-thick cedar benderboard; lower-quality material is likely to crack or split. It may need to be special-ordered or milled, but it is worth the extra cost. It easily bends to wrap around the curve.

STAIRS. Install stringers that rest on a solid surface. Attach decking-board treads, and allow them to run wild on each side. Use the outer compass to mark the treads for cutting at the same curve as the decking.

RAILING. Have a railing fabricator measure and install the railing. The railing posts should be attached with screws driven into joists—not just the decking.

BECAUSE KATWIJK INSTALLS DECK-ING with wide ⅜-in. gaps between boards, his black hidden fasteners are actually a part of the deck's appearance.

IF YOU ARE WORKING with a railing fabricator, make sure the railing posts are attached to the deck framing, not just the decking. The curve of the railing complements the curve of the decking.

DOUBLE CURVED

TWO NEARLY CIRCULAR DECKS AND A CLASSICAL-STYLE PERGOLA
COMBINE TO CREATE A SERENE AND JUST SLIGHTLY FANCIFUL BACK-
YARD SETTING.

A PERGOLA makes a strong design statement, especially for Katwijk who avoids vertical design elements. This pergola is made entirely of synthetic materials, so it is easy to maintain.

DESIGN CONSIDERATIONS

This backyard has some nice decorative elements, but the owners wanted a deck that would add a stunning touch. The elements—round deck surfaces combined with an ornate pergola that looks as though it belongs on a Greek portico—might not sound like they go together, but by using sophisticated design software that shows how things will look, Katwijk gained confidence to combine the two. It helps that the vertical skirting boards under the decking look a bit like fluted pillars themselves.

The decking and skirting is composite in a muted color. The decking is run at several different angles on the two decks and the short stairs.

SMALL DECK AND PERGOLA. The owners did not want to cook on the deck; they just wanted dining and lounging areas. The smaller deck is off the kitchen door. Its size and the positions of the pergola's columns perfectly frame a dining area, with ample room for a round four-chair table; a larger table could fit in, as well. For a large gathering, people eat buffet style.

The pergola is in an old style, but is constructed of modern synthetic materials that are easy to maintain. The pillars have a rough "sand-finished" texture that mimics the look of old stone; they are easy to clean with a damp cloth. The horizontal pieces on top have a glossy finish that barely requires cleaning; rainfall or an occasional hosing will usually keep them looking good.

LARGE DECK. Two steps down from the dining deck is a larger deck made just for relaxing. The owners did not want built-in planters or benches. But Katwijk did add a tasteful decorative element, made with four tiles framed by composite lumber of a different color.

CONSTRUCTION TECHNIQUES

Because some of the framing members will touch or come near the ground, use treated lumber rated for ground contact or in-ground use. Be sure to apply sealer to any cut ends before installing the boards.

FOOTINGS AND LEDGER. Measure from the house to determine the locations for the footings, and dig holes as required. Where a line of footings will support a beam, use a string line to be sure they are in a straight row.

On a very low deck, the beams may sink below grade. Dig channels for the beams so that they will not touch soil. These beams may rest directly on top of the footings, with no posts. In that case, the footings must be installed at precise heights. (See page 165.)

Dig the holes, and place the concrete and the cast-concrete pier. As an alternative, you can place a concrete tube form in the hole; pour the concrete; and insert post anchors into the wet concrete.

Install the ledger and any flashing or standoffs, following local codes to ensure it will support the deck and will keep water from collecting and damaging the house.

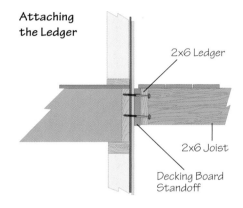

Attaching the Ledger

2x6 Ledger

2x6 Joist

Decking Board Standoff

PLAN VIEW

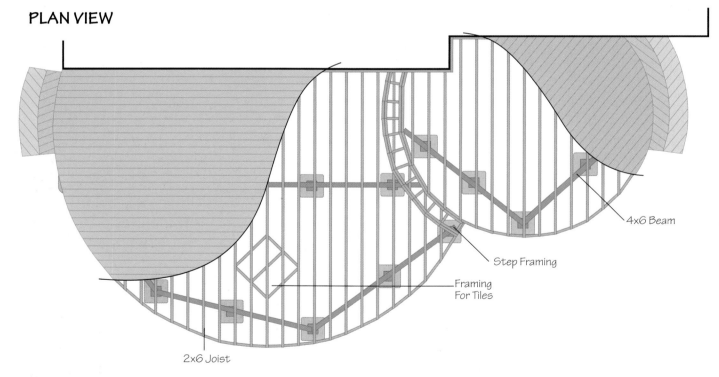

4x6 Beam

Step Framing

Framing For Tiles

2x6 Joist

MATERIALS USED FOR THIS DECK

Framing (all treated)	4x4 posts 4x6 beams 2x6 ledger and joists 2x12 stair stringers	Decking and Skirting	5/4x6 composite decking
		Overhead	Fiberglass columns, beams, rafters, and top pieces

LEDGER WITH STANDOFFS

HERE IS THE METHOD KATWIJK USES for most of his ledgers. It is designed to allow rainwater and wet debris to flow behind the ledger so that it can dry out. Check with your building department; they may require other methods and fasteners. Snap or draw a layout line on the house's siding to mark the top of the ledger; the decking that will be installed on top of the ledger should be an inch or two below the sill.

1. Using composite decking or other rot-proof material, cut a number of short pieces, called standoffs, as long as the ledger is wide. Cut the top at a slight V so water cannot collect on top. Apply caulk to the back of each piece just before installing it.

2. Attach the standoffs every 12 or 16 inches, their tops aligned with the chalk-line marking for the top of the ledger.

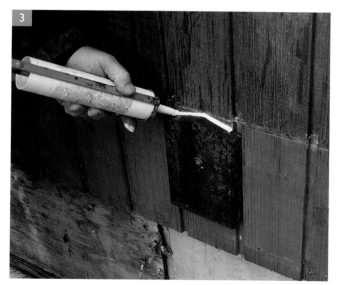

3. Caulk the top of each standoff to ensure water cannot infiltrate behind it and damage the house's siding.

4. Fasten the ledger to the house using screws driven through the standoffs. Note that these screws should be driven at a slight upward angle so any water that wicks into the screw's hole can flow back away from the house. Katwijk prefers to use extra-strong screws with ¼-in.-wide shanks made specifically for attaching ledgers. Less water wicks along these screws than would wick along thicker ½-in. screws.

FRAMING. Build framing for the lower, larger deck first; then build the upper level. The lower level will support the stair between the two levels.

Use a transit level or other type of level to determine the height of the posts; their tops will be one beam's width below the bottom of the joists. Cut and install the posts onto the post anchors. Add post caps, and attach beams on top of the posts. You may cut the beams to length now, or let them run wild and cut them later.

Lay out on the ledger and the beams for the joist locations. Install the joists, attaching them to the ledger via joist hangers and resting them on top of the beams. Allow the joists to run wild; you will cut them off later. Attach joists to the beams with straps or angle-driven nails or screws.

Install joists for a curved deck using the techniques shown on pages 151–152. Use a pencil-and-tape-measure compass to mark the tops of the joists for the curve, and draw squared lines on either side of each board. Use a small chain saw (work carefully) to cut the joist ends at the correct bevels. Also use the chain saw to cut the blocking pieces that fit between the joists.

Determine how you will install the columns for the pergola, and install blocking pieces between the joists as needed.

DECKING AND TILES. Determine where the tile pattern will go, and install angled blocking pieces as needed to support the tiles, the different-colored decking border, and the boards that will butt against the border. Follow manufacturer's directions for installing braces that support the decking tiles. Install the tiles and the border before running the regular decking.

Attach the decking on the lower level parallel with the house. Katwijk keeps the piece nearest the house at least ⅜ inch away from the siding, for drainage. Let the decking run wild past the framing. Use the compass to mark the decking for a circular cut; it should run about 2 inches past the framing. Install the upper decking at an angle.

The skirting is made of short decking pieces. On a low deck like this, there is no need to build framing to attach skirting at the bottom. Katwijk digs a trench and buries the skirting two inches or so in the ground; there is no possibility of this material rotting.

STAIRS. For the step between the two levels, build a curved framing section with short joists. For the stairs on each side that leave the deck, use stair stringers that rest on a concrete or paver surface.

THE OVERHEAD. The columns, beams, rafters, and top pieces are all made of fiberglass. These days you can get elements like this in composite, PVC, aluminum, and polyurethane, but Katwijk says fiberglass is the strongest and most stable. Many companies advertise on the Web, and have programs that help you assemble all the parts you need for a custom creation.

The system shown here uses a long threaded rod that runs from the top of the column down through the deck framing to secure the column. It must run through a piece of blocking fastened between the joists—not just the decking. Below the framing and on top of the column, position a metal plate, and tighten screws to fasten the threaded rod.

Slip the beams into slots on top of the columns (in this case, one of the beams attaches to the house at one end) and use the supplied hardware to fasten the beams. Lay out on top of the beams for evenly spaced rafters, and fasten them with small stainless-steel brackets and screws. Attach the top pieces by driving stainless-steel screws down into rafters.

Elevation

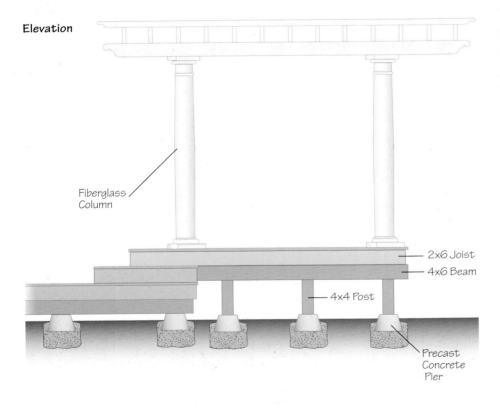

Fiberglass Column

2x6 Joist

4x6 Beam

4x4 Post

Precast Concrete Pier

THIS FIBERGLASS PERGOLA, above, should last for years with minimal care. As shown, although awkward, the columns are easy to move into place. Note: there are only three columns here because one edge of one support beam is attached to the house.

SECURE THE COLUMNS, right, to the framing under the decking. This system has a threaded rod that runs from the top of the column through the deck framing.

FLOATING PLATFORMS

FIVE SMALL, RECTANGULAR DECKS, OR PLATFORMS, DROP DOWN A HILL
IN A MANNER THAT LOOKS HALF RANDOM AND HALF PLANNED. THE
PLATFORMS VARY IN SIZE AND DECK ORIENTATION, AND END AT A SPA.

HOVERING PLAT-FORMS appear to spill down the slope of this yard. Because the decking is so close to the ground, Katwijk and the client decided on composite material for the exposed surfaces.

DESIGN CONSIDERATIONS

Though the deck serves practical uses, artistic design is at the fore here. The effect is fanciful, as if a giant's child had left some building blocks lying around or a group of rafts bumped into each other on a river.

THE PLATFORMS. All the platforms are installed as close to ground level as possible so that they feel like part of the landscape. There is no straight path from the house to the large deck with the spa; you must meander around a little clump of flowers. This helps define the deck as a place that is part of nature and separated from the serious world.

The small uppermost platform functions as an entry porch. Two steps lead down to another platform similar in size. Off to the side, a 9-× 7-foot platform has just enough room for some lounge chairs and a clear pathway. After another small platform, you reach the main deck, a medium-size affair with a centrally located spa.

BENCH AND SPA. A single, modest bench offers a relaxing spot for bathers and forms a barrier at the deck's highest point above grade. Steps on the side of the spa offer more seating possibilities. There are also stairs near the bench.

Katwijk often raises a spa 16 inches or so above the deck and provides a bench alongside it. However, this spa's lip is just above deck level, in keeping with the low-to-the-ground approach of the whole deck.

THE DECKING. The neutral tones of the gray composite decking are in harmony with a gray-sided house and the often-cloudy Northwestern skies. The gray highlights splashes of color given by the flowers, toys, and furniture. In other settings, a wood or even greenish tone might be preferred. Of course, low-maintenance, rot-resistant composite decking is a good choice where a deck is this low to ground that is sometimes muddy.

CONSTRUCTION TECHNIQUES

Of course, your yard probably slopes differently from this one, so you will need to adjust the sizes and positions of your platforms. Use treated lumber rated for ground contact or in-ground use wherever joists or beams will come near the soil.

PLANNING THE HEIGHTS. A 2x6 joist topped with 5/4 (1-inch-thick) decking makes for a 6½-inch vertical rise—which is a comfortable step height. So stacking one finished deck on top of another is an easy way to get good step heights.

To be comfortable to walk on, each step—whether on a set of stairs or a step from one deck to the next—should be the same rise (vertical distance). To achieve this, Katwijk builds the top and bottom decks first, and carefully calculates their levels so

PLAN VIEW

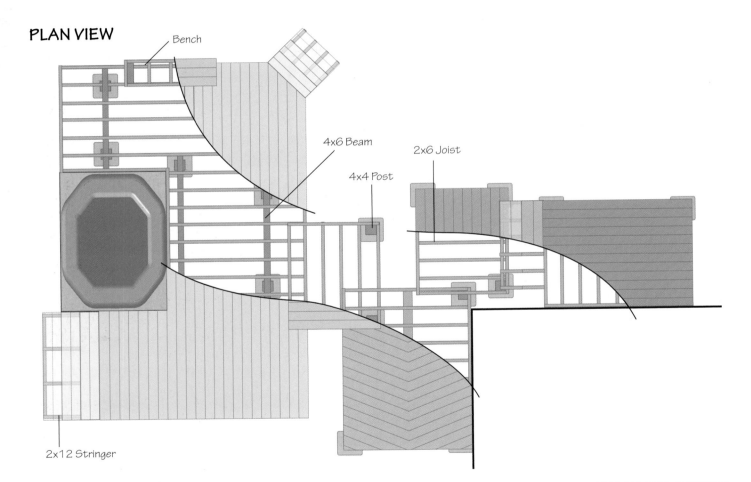

Bench

4x6 Beam

4x4 Post

2x6 Joist

2x12 Stringer

MATERIALS USED FOR THIS DECK

Framing (all treated)	4x4 posts 4x6 beams (lower deck only) 2x6 ledger and joists 2x12 for stair stringers	Decking and Fascia	5/4x6 composite decking
		Bench	4x10 treated supports 2x4 treated framing pieces 5/4x6 composite decking for the seat and fascia

WORKING WITH TREATED LUMBER

KATWIJK FINDS THAT THE TREATED LUMBER in his area often needs extra protection. When you cut through it, you can see clearly that the green treatment soaks through only an inch or so.

So Katwijk makes sure to soak all cut lumber ends with a penetrating sealer/preservative that has a proven track record in his area. A sealer with a good dose of copper is recommended.

When possible, dip the cut end into a bucket filled with the sealer, and let it soak in for a few minutes. If that is not possible, use a brush to apply several coats of sealer.

UNEVEN PENETRATION OF TREATMENT

EVEN PENETRATION OF TREATMENT

all the step rises between will come out the same. If you are less sure of your skills, you could build (or at least frame) the platforms one at a time and in sequence, stacking one on top of the other—or slipping one under the other—as you go.

The top platform is attached to the house just under a doorsill. In most areas, this platform should be positioned either about 1 inch below the sill or one full step down.

PLATFORM FRAMING. Platforms that are very small probably don't need beams, but check with your building department to be sure. You may need to double up the header joists and add joist hangers; this turns the header into a flush beam.

An experienced deck builder like Katwijk will use a transit level to precisely locate all the heights and positions of the posts, install the posts, and then build the framing. For a do-it-yourselfer, here is a method that takes more time but does not call for precise calculations: build the frames for each of the four smaller platforms on a flat surface, such as a driveway or on the ground near where they will go. Check that they

are square as you build, and take care to keep all the top surfaces flush with each other. A nail or screw gun makes this work easier; if you pound nails by hand, the structure will wobble more as you build. Because the platform frames are small, you and a helper can easily lift and move them.

Where the platforms will stack on top of each other, tack scrap pieces of decking on the framing so that you get the correct thickness. Put the platform frames in place, some stacked on each other, and temporarily support them so they are level.

Elevation

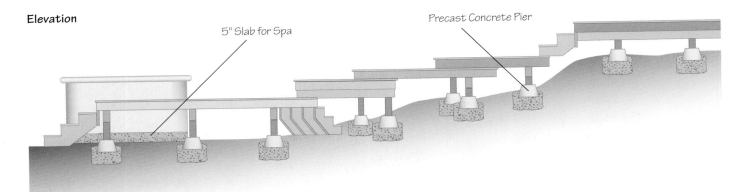

5" Slab for Spa

Precast Concrete Pier

FOOTINGS AND POSTS. Once you are certain the platform frames are where you want them, mark the ground for the footing holes; the posts will attach to the inside corners of the frames.

Dig holes and pour concrete as required by your building department. (For Katwijk's method, see opposite.)

With platforms, you can cut the posts off after the framing is completed. Cut all the posts longer than they need to be. Position the framing, and temporarily support it so it is level. Slip the posts into the post anchors on the footings, and adjust their position so they are snug against the inside corner of the framing. Check the posts for plumb, and fasten them to the post anchor and to the framing.

Use a reciprocating saw or handsaw to cut the posts flush with the top of the framing. Install the decking.

SPA AND LOWER DECK. A spa typically rests on a concrete slab; follow the manufacturer's directions. You will need to bring electrical power and water to the spa and provide an access panel so you can service the pump and other components as needed.

Build the lower deck in the standard way: install footings, then posts, then beams. Build the framing on top of the beams.

THE BENCH. Building this bench could hardly be easier. Cut two pieces of 4x10 cedar to the desired height of the bench, minus 1 inch (the thick-

ness of the decking). Build a simple 2x4 frame around the top of the 4x10s. Cut and install decking so it overhangs about 1½ inches on all sides. Wrap the outside of the 2x4 framing with decking or fascia board.

Bench Detail

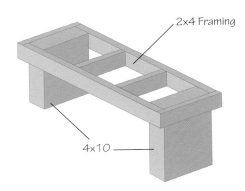

2x4 Framing

4x10

SPAS USUALLY REST on a concrete pad. The spa at left rises a few inches above the decking. Note how the decking is cut to follow the curve of the spa.

A SMALL BENCH, right, is made of cedar supports and a 2x4 frame covered with decking material.

INSTALLING DECK FOOTINGS

THIS METHOD WORKS and is approved in Katwijk's area, where the ground is usually damp and does not freeze in the winter. In other areas, you may be required to dig a hole below the frostline and pour concrete for either an in-ground or an aboveground post.

1. Dig a square hole, 16 in. square and 16 in. deep. Tamp the bottom firm with a 2x4. Pour a bag or two of dry concrete mix into the hole. (In dryer areas, you will need to mix and pour wet concrete, and you will likely need to dig a deeper hole.)

2. Set a precast concrete pier onto the dry concrete, and twist as you press it down firmly. Check that its metal post anchor is correctly aligned.

3. Pour a half bag of concrete around the pier.

4. Where there will be three or more footings/posts supporting the same beam, stretch a mason's line between the outer piers to ensure that the inner piers are perfectly lined up.

5. Add soil to fill the hole around the pier, and step on it until it's firm. If the ground is damp, the concrete will form and set overnight.

DECK BUILDERS INC.

KEYHOLE SHAPE

WITH ITS SIMPLE, ELEGANT SHAPE, THIS DECK BLENDS NICELY WITH THE FLOWING CURVES OF THE LANDSCAPING AND PROVIDES A PLEASANT PLACE TO RELAX UNDER A FLOWERING TREE. A MODEST SCREEN PROVIDES A BIT OF PRIVACY WITHOUT MAKING THE PLACE FEEL ENCLOSED.

DESIGN CONSIDERATIONS

The owners do their serious outdoor cooking and dining on the other side of the house. Here, they just wanted a nice-looking place for relaxing and enjoying the landscape.

A DECK LIKE A PATIO. The yard here is almost perfectly flat and is only slightly below the door, so the deck would be at patio level. The owners could have installed a paver or stone surface, but they liked the feel of natural wood. But like so many people these days, they did not want the maintenance demands of most natural wood. Low-maintenance composite decking in a beige wood tone struck the right chord for them.

The lawn is cut in curved sections, so a curved deck was a natural complement. The deck's front edge parallels the lawn for about a third of its circumference, then curves back toward the house to become its own place.

THE SCREEN. The owners were in a slightly awkward situation: a neighbor's patio doors look directly onto the deck, and they sometimes found themselves face to face. They didn't want to build an unfriendly fence, so they opted for a strategically positioned privacy screen. About 12 feet long, it takes up less than one-fourth of the deck's circumference.

The screen is a one-of-a-kind work of art that parties on both sides can appreciate. Vertical slats, made of beautiful stained cedar one-by, alternate in an orderly pattern. The 1-inch spaces between the slats let the light through while hiding most of the view.

NESTLED AGAINST THE HOUSE this small deck serves as a escape for the owners. Because the deck is in full view of a neighbor's house, the screen offers a friendly barrier. Cedar slats alternate widths to let in light while providing privacy.

Elevation

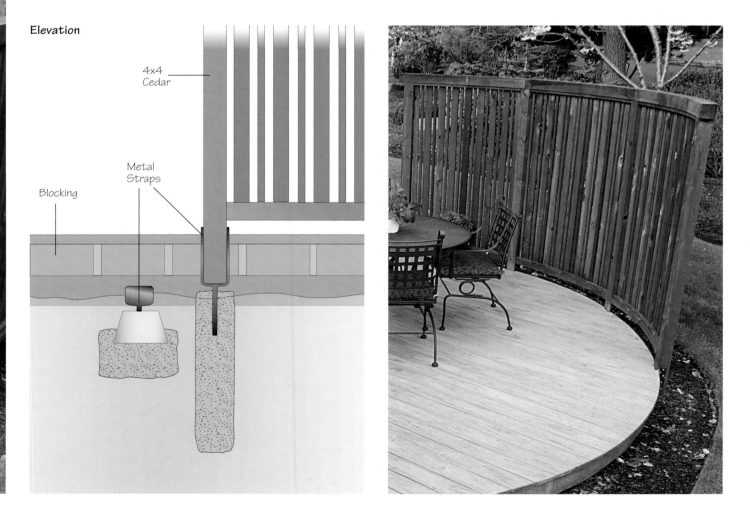

4x4 Cedar

Metal Straps

Blocking

CONSTRUCTION TECHNIQUES

A very low deck calls for some excavating and for some special techniques, but it requires no special skills. There are no posts; the beams rest directly on concrete footings. Use good-quality lumber rated for in-ground use wherever it may come into contact with the soil.

PLAN VIEW

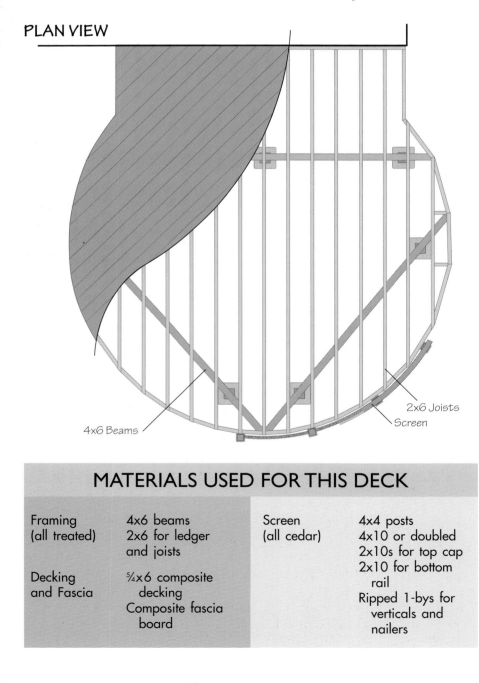

4x6 Beams

2x6 Joists
Screen

LEDGER, LAYOUT, AND EXCAVATION. Start by installing the ledger board according to local codes. Mark the ledger with layout lines for the joist locations; then drive approved fasteners to secure the ledger.

If the deck must be built so low that even the joists will be below grade, it's a good idea to excavate away some soil for the entire site; it is not practical to dig trenches for each joist.

Measure out from the ledger to determine where the beams will go. The beam nearest the house is parallel with the ledger, and the other two beams are at 45-degree angles to it. Use a transit level, a water level, or a carpenter's level set atop a long board to determine how deeply you will need to excavate for the beams. Even if you use very good treated lumber, aim to keep all boards at least 3 inches away from soil.

If you use 2x6 joists and 4x6 beams (both of which are 5½ inches wide), the beams will be 11 inches below the top of the ledger, so dig trenches that are at least 14 inches deeper than the top of the ledger. Dig trenches a few inches longer than they need to be so that you can run the beams a little wild. Use your foot, and then a 4x4 or 2x4, to tamp the bottoms of the trenches firm.

FOOTINGS AND BEAMS. Cut the beams a few inches longer than they need to be, and set them in the trenches. Using a level, make sure they will be at least 3 inches above the soil when they are at the correct height (with their tops at the bottom of the ledger). Temporarily support the beams at the right height, and measure to see how high each footing will need to be in order to support them.

Remove the beams, and dig holes for the footings. If you're using Katwijk's footing method, with a precast pier sitting in dry concrete mix, buy piers with post anchors made to support a four-by beam. Pour dry concrete mix into each of the holes, and set piers on top. Place the

MATERIALS USED FOR THIS DECK

| Framing (all treated) | 4x6 beams 2x6 for ledger and joists | Screen (all cedar) | 4x4 posts 4x10 or doubled 2x10s for top cap 2x10 for bottom rail Ripped 1-bys for verticals and nailers |
| Decking and Fascia | ⁵⁄₄x6 composite decking Composite fascia board | | |

SOLID 4X6 BEAMS support all of Katwijk's decks. In this case, he excavated to install the footings and beams and keep the deck close to the ground.

Cutting Piece for Screen

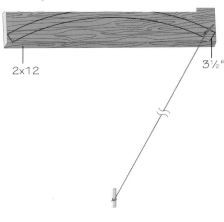

2x12   3½"

beam on the pier, and use a level to see that it is level and at the correct height. Adjust as needed by adding or removing concrete mix around the piers.

If you will pour concrete into tube forms, dig holes and place the tubes. A 4x6 beam will be too heavy to set on the tubes, so test for correct height using a two-by board. Take into account the height of the beam anchor you will insert into the wet concrete. To ensure that a tube stays at the correct height, lay a pair of short 2x4 braces against it on the ground, and drive screws from the inside of the form into the 2x4s. Pour the concrete, and set the anchors, using a level and a string line to make sure they are correctly aligned and at the right height.

Allow the concrete to cure, and set the beams into the anchors, letting them run wild on either side.

JOISTS. Mark the beams for the positions of the joists. Install joists, longer than they need to be, by attaching to the ledger with joist hangers and using straps or angle-driven fasteners at the beams.

Install joists for a curved deck using the techniques shown on pages 151–152. Use a pencil-and-tape-measure compass to mark the tops of the joists for the curve. Use a circular saw to cut the joist ends and the blocking pieces to fit between the

joists. You will be constantly changing the bevel on your circular saw as you make these cuts. At each side of the circle you will need to cut short blocking pieces at right angles to the joist, then install blocking pieces between them.

Dig holes for footings that will support the screen posts. (It's best to do this after the curved framing is complete). The footings should be at least 2 feet deep and have long metal anchors to support the posts laterally.

MOISTURE PROTECTION. In many areas, it is common to install the decking, then the fascia. However, because Katwijk is so concerned about moisture collecting between the fascia and the framing, he installs the fascia; then he covers the perimeter framing with strips of peel-and-stick roofing or flexible flashing.

For the curved fascia, you may be able to use ½-inch-thick fascia board, often available in the same color as the decking. Here, however, the fascia board was not available, so Katwijk hired a mill to rip-cut decking pieces to half thickness—producing a very flexible board.

DECKING. Run the decking at an angle to the house. Start near the middle of the deck, and work outward in both directions. (For Katwijk's hidden fastener system, see page 176.) Allow the decking to over-

hang the fascia by at least 2 inches; use the tape-measure-and-pencil compass to mark for a circular cut, so they will overhang by 1½ inches.

THE SCREEN. Cut and set the posts in the post anchors. Temporarily brace them so they stay plumb as you work. Use a power nailer to fasten the rest of the screen; hand nailing will make it wobble too much while you work.

The top cap seen in the photo on page 167 was cut from massive 4x10s; Katwijk hired a mill worker to do this. You can get much the same effect by cutting two pieces out of 2x10s or 2x12s, then stacking them on top with overlapping joints. Mark the two-by using the same compass you used for marking the decking; then cut using a jigsaw or a circular saw. For the bottom layer, cut the pieces to length so they rest on the middle of the posts. For the upper layer, cut different lengths and fasten to the lower layer. Cut the bottom rail out of 2x10, using the same technique.

Rip pieces of clear cedar one-by to ¾ inch or so, and fasten them to the back side of the top and bottom rails. The vertical pieces will snug against these as you fasten them. Use a table saw to cut the vertical slats to the desired widths—here, 3 inches and 1 inch. Fasten the verticals; then attach more ¾-inch one-by to the face at the top and bottom.

TILING A DECK

OVER THE YEARS a number of manufacturers have come up with products and systems to produce a tile, or at least a tile appearance, on a raised deck surface. Beware: many of these systems have failed, resulting in cracked tiles. Choose a product with a proven track record in your area. The method shown here uses a fiberglass web substrate to create a surface that is very rigid, so you can install almost any type of exterior-grade tile on top of it. Here, we show a natural stone tile. Make sure that the tile you choose can survive your winters.

1. Construct deck framing that is strong and rigid. Here, 2x8 joists span only 4 ft. or so, and the stair stringers rest on a solid base. To protect the bottoms of the stringers from rot, Katwijk often lays pieces of ½-in. composite fascia board between the base and the stringer bottoms. Here, the risers are covered with fascia board rather than tiles.

3. Plan for an attractive tile layout, with no narrow slivers at the sides, front, or against the house. Use a wet-cutting masonry saw to cut the tiles, and lay a number of tiles in place before you start setting them in adhesive.

4. Clean the tile backs, and apply adhesive as recommended by the manufacturer of the webbing. Here, the tile is first cleaned with de-natured alcohol. A small amount of adhesive is squeezed onto the tile using a caulk gun, then spread with a notched trowel. More adhesive is then applied with the caulk gun.

5. Press the tiles into place. Here, the tiles are butted snugly together. You may choose to use plastic tiling spacers to maintain gaps between the tiles. (No grout can be applied to the joint between the tiles.)

6. For tricky cuts, such as this a curved edge, hold a tile in place and scribe from below using a pencil. A stone tile like this should not overhang the fascia by more than ¼ in.; stronger tiles may overhang farther.

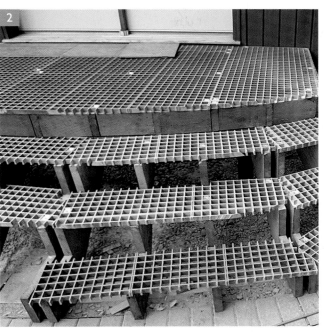

2. Use a circular saw to cut pieces of fiberglass webbing to fit snugly in place. The material comes with metal clips that fit into holes in the webbing; drive stainless-steel screws through the clips to fasten the webbing to the framing.

EXTERIOR TILE DECKS AND STEPS require a rigid substrate that will not shift and cause the tile to crack.

PAVERS AND GLASS PAVERS

ANOTHER TYPE OF DECK "TILE" actually uses thick concrete pavers. These pavers are tinted to look like tiles, but they are strong enough to span across joists that are spaced 24 inches apart. The joists must be four-bys rather than two-bys. Katwijk adds a layer of torch-down roofing on top of the joists for cushioning. Here, some of the pavers are actually made of thick glass to add light to an area below.

A DECK PLUS A SUNKEN LOUNGE

A DECK WITH A WIDE EXPANSE HAS AT ITS PROW A LOWERED SEATING AREA WITH BENCHES. THIS MAKES FOR TWO COMPLETELY DIFFERENT-FEELING SPACES, ONE INTIMATE AND THE OTHER OPEN.

LITTLE DETAILS can greatly improve a design. At right, the portion of railing near the grill is topped with a cap that is about 17 in. wide, giving the cook a place to set down plates, ingredients, and cooking equipment.

RAILINGS THAT BLEND into the surroundings is what Katwijk strives for with his railing system. When the background is dense vegetation, he uses black rods because they seem to disappear into the scenery.

DESIGN CONSIDERATIONS

The owners wanted a large deck for occasional parties, but they also wanted to have a place where they could retreat and enjoy their yard with one or two friends or family members. The deck addresses both needs beautifully.

MAIN DECK. The deck as a whole is actually basically square, but it doesn't feel squarish because it is tilted 45 degrees to the house. Because the sunken room cuts into the main space, it divides the deck into two areas. Party goers tend to congregate in three main areas—the two main deck spaces and the sunken area.

A small bump-out on one side holds a medium-size barbecue grill. To the right as you face the grill, a simple food prep table is made by increasing the width of the rail cap to about 17 inches. This leaves ample room for placing bowls, plates, and cooking implements.

SUNKEN ROOM. The sunken lounge is about 12 feet from the kitchen door—far enough to feel a bit secluded but not out of the loop. When seated at the curved-back benches, you find yourself oriented

toward other lounge members and the view of Puget Sound.

Stairs on each side of the benches add seating possibilities, and an end table can be used for plants or magazines and drinks.

RAILING. This is Katwijk's signature thin-rod railing, designed to be nearly invisible while at the same time complying with safety codes. You'll find instructions for building this railing on page 177.

Katwijk installs the thinnest possible rods for maximum see-through-ability. If the background is mainly vegetation, as here, he uses black rods, which virtually disappear against a dark background. Where the view is mostly lake or sea, he uses unpainted stainless steel, which shimmers and blends with the water.

CONSTRUCTION TECHNIQUES

PLAN VIEW

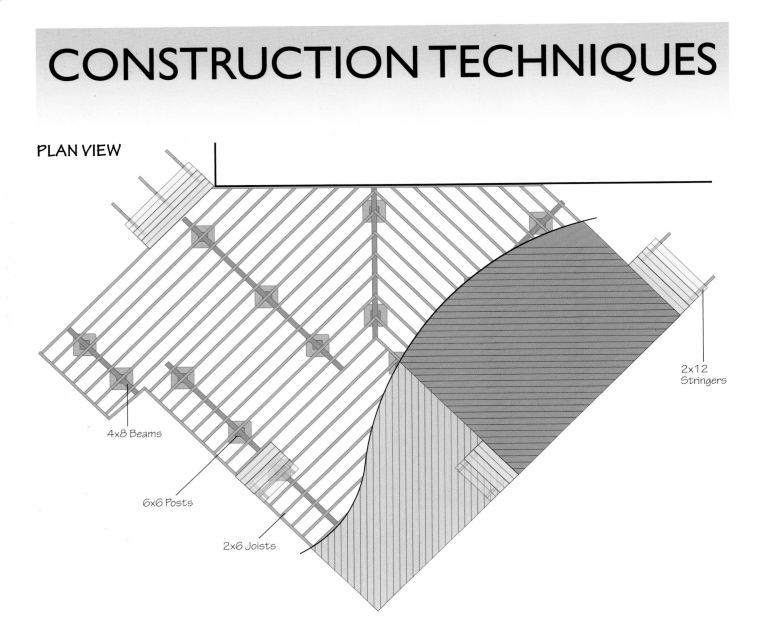

2x12 Stringers

4x8 Beams

6x6 Posts

2x6 Joists

MATERIALS USED FOR THIS DECK

Framing (all treated)	6x6 posts 4x4 braces 4x8 beams 2x6 ledger and joists 2x12 stair stringers	
Decking and Fascia	⁵⁄₄x6 composite decking	
Railing	Treated 4x4 posts Composite post sleeves 2x4 composite top and bottom rails ⁵⁄₄x6 decking for rail cap ¼" powder-coated steel rods	

Bench	Treated 4 x 16-ft. (or 2x12 and 2x8)
	   vertical supports
	Treated 2x4 framing
	⁵⁄₄x6 composite decking
	   for visible parts	

Because he wanted to lessen the number of footings, Katwijk used 4x8 beams rather than his usual 4x6s. (The wider the structural member, the longer the distance it can span.) Because the deck is high, 6x6 posts were required instead of his usual 4x4s.

FOOTINGS, POSTS, AND BEAMS.
This deck was built fairly high and on a sloped site, which presents layout challenges. One option—used by the other builders in this book—is to build temporarily supported joist and ledger framing first; then hang the beam and the posts from it. However, because of moisture concerns Katwijk uses heavy four-by beams and footings that rise above the ground, so it is more practical to build from the ground up.

Fortunately, under-joist beams do not have to be precisely positioned; often, they can be off by as much as 6 inches and they will still support the joists just fine.

Install a ledger that complies with local codes, and mark it with the locations of the joists. Here's a do-it-yourselfer method: referencing the framing plan for the post locations, have one helper hold a straight board with a level on top of it so it rests on the ledger. Have another helper check that the board is at a right angle to the ledger. Once you are at

THE FIRST STEP IN FRAMING is to set the posts and install the beams. These are 6x6 posts and 4x8 beams.

the correct distance and angle from the house, dangle a plumb bob (or a chalk-line box) from the board to locate the posthole position on the ground.

For each row of three or more posts, just mark for the outer holes. Once you start setting the outer footings, string lines between them to mark for the inner holes.

Install footings and post anchors as required, and allow the concrete to set. Use a transit level or other level to determine the post heights—one beam's thickness below the bottom of the ledger. Cut and install the posts. Attach special post caps designed for a 6x6 post and a four-by beam, and install the beams. You can allow the beams to run wild and cut them to length later.

JOISTS. Use braces to temporarily support the posts and beams to keep them plumb while you work. One center joist runs atop the center-angled beam. Mark the beam tops with the positions of the joists, which run at an angle to the house. Attach joists to the ledger using angled joist hangers, and use straps or angle-driven fasteners to attach them to the beams; let them run wild. At the front ends of the framing, use a chalk line to mark the tops of the joists; then mark for square cuts, and cut each with a circular saw. Attach a header (also called a rim joist) to the cut ends.

DECKING. Run the decking and install it, perhaps using the fastener system shown on page 176.

Elevation

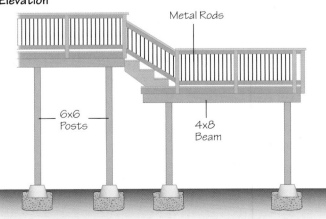

6x6 Posts

Metal Rods

4x8 Beam

INSTALL JOISTS AND DECKING. It is often best to let these run wild and then cut to size later.

KATWIJK'S HIDDEN-FASTENER SYSTEM

KATWIJK USES THIS METHOD for both composite and wood decking. It works well if, like Katwijk, you leave ⅜-inch gaps between decking boards. Such a larger-than-usual gap allows debris and moisture to easily fall between the cracks and prolongs the life of a deck in a damp area. It also makes it easier to clean the deck.

To get the materials, contact a company that makes washers and screws. Order a box of 1-inch stainless-steel fender washers and a box of 2-inch stainless-steel #8 screws anodized black in color. It may take some calling around, and you may need to buy more screws and washers than you will need, but the cost will probably still be less than using standard decking clips or other types of hidden fasteners.

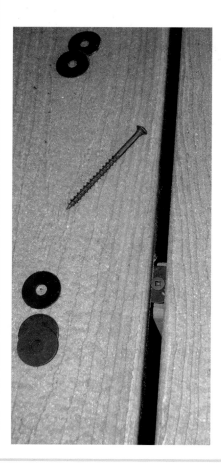

1. Equip a router with a ⅟₁₆-in. single-kerf side-cutting bit, and adjust it so it cuts into the middle of the decking's thickness; test on scrap pieces to make sure. Position the decking where it will go. Tilt it up, and cut grooves in the edges of the decking that will be above the joists.

2. You will need to face-screw one side of the first decking piece. Slip a washer into the groove at each joist.

3. Rout grooves in the next decking board, and push it into position so the washer is inserted into grooves in both boards. Drive screws through the washers and into the joists.

THIN-ROD RAILING

CHECK WITH YOUR BUILDING DEPARTMENT to make sure this railing will meet local codes. Because it's out of the ordinary, you may need to convince an inspector that it's strong. From a metal shop, order ¼-inch rods. Order either powder-coated rods made of cold-rolled steel, or uncoated stainless-steel rods. You can cut the rods to length yourself (though stainless steel can be difficult), or order them precut. The length of the rods depends on the railing design and height.

DECK BUILDERS INC.

1. In the railing shown above, the rails are made of simple 2×4 composite material. However, many manufacturers do not supply simple composite 2×4s; their rails are made to go with other railing components. Use a table saw or circular saw with a rip guide (here, a pair of locking pliers is used) to modify the rails.

2. After installing the posts, cut the top and bottom rails to fit between them. Mark the rails with the locations of evenly spaced rods, no more than 4 in. apart. Drill ⁵⁄₁₆-in. holes into the marks you made. Drill all the way through the top rail and halfway through the bottom rail. Drill the holes straight.

3. On a stair rail, the rods need to be installed at an angle. To identify this angle, place a board atop the stairway. Hold a speed square against it with a small level on top (left). When you achieve level, the square will show you the angle at which to drill the holes. To drill angled holes, cut a small piece of wood or decking at that angle, and use a drill to make a groove along one edge (right). Use this jig as a guide for drilling the holes.

4. Attach the rails to the posts. Slip each rod down through the top rail and into the bottom rail. Add the rail cap.

CURVED DECKING

SETTING A CURVED DECKING DESIGN

Composite decking can be bent into curves to create all sorts of pattern on a decking surface. However, as the next four pages show, creating an ornate curved design calls for careful planning, special tools, and plenty of patience.

Though it looks like there are all sorts of arcs in this design, Katwijk designed it to use only two types of curves: the white circle has a radius of 6 feet, and all the other pieces have a radius of 6 feet 6 inches. Once a series of boards have been bent to those radii, they can be cut to length to create the pattern.

I. FRAMING AND MAKING THE FORM

Start by building standard deck framing. Where the curved pieces run parallel with joists, they will need blocking pieces, so they are supported every 12 inches by a framing member. Use an accurate scale drawing of the design as your guide.

2. Cut a series of scrap two-bys to the radius against which you will form the decking. This is best done using a circular saw equipped with a special curve-cutting blade. (A jigsaw will not produce as smooth a curve, and you cannot use it later, when you cut the decking.)

1. Framing pieces must support both the curved pieces and the regular decking. This is best done before installing the regular decking. Stretch strings across the top of the framing to represent the center lines of the decorative sections. Then use a tape-measure-and-pencil compass to mark the tops of the joists to show where the curved pieces will go. Mark both sides of each curved decking piece.

Expect to spend plenty of time installing the blocking pieces. Hold boards in place; mark them for the angles of the cuts; and cut with a small chain saw. Using a power nailer or screw gun, attach the blocking pieces carefully, with their tops perfectly flush with the tops of joists. (Hand nailing is not recommended and it will not be easy.)

3. Place a sheet of plywood on a flat surface, and use a compass to mark it with the desired radius. Position radius-cut two-bys along the line, and fasten them with screws. Place other radius-cut pieces nearby, so you can attach them later when you bend the board.

2. HEATING A DECKING BOARD

Before a composite board can be bent severely, it must be heated. One method is to put the board in a large plastic pipe and then direct a construction-type heater at it, but that takes a very long time and is not reliable. A blanket heater like the one shown here is expensive, but really does the job.

1. Lay the blanket on top of fiberglass insulation on a flat surface, and position the controller nearby. Place the board on top of the blanket's heating strip.

2. Drill a hole in the side of the decking, and insert the controller's thermometer probe. The board should be heated to about 265°F.

3. Lay a fiberglass batt on top of the board; plug the controller into an outlet; and program the controller to heat the board to the desired temperature.

CURVED DECKING (cont'd.)

3. FORMING THE ARC

You have only a short time until the board cools, so make sure the form is ready before you lift the board.

1. Once the correct temperature is reached, you'll need several helpers wearing protective gloves to help carry the board, which will be quite flexible.

2. Set the heated board onto the plywood, and press it against the radius-cut boards. Work quickly but thoroughly, so the board is tight at all points.

4. Sometimes the heating process produces bubbles in the decking. Direct a heat gun toward the bubble until it softens; then press with a gloved thumb to deflate it.

3. Place the other radius-cut boards against the other side of the heated board; press into place; and use a series of clamps to tighten them.

5. Once it cools, the finished decking board is stable and can be easily transported to the deck.

DECK BUILDERS INC.

4. CUT AND PLACE THE BENT DECKING

Marking and cutting the decking must be done accurately, so attempt this only if you are certain of your skills.

1. Use a pencil-and tape-measure compass to mark the intersections of the curved boards. (Because the boards will not be perfectly bent, they will not follow these lines exactly.)

2. Place the bent boards where they will go; they will overlap now, and will be cut to length later. Drive screws to fasten the regular decking a few inches on each side of the curved boards.

3. Make sure that the curved boards are exactly where they will go, and tack them in place so they will not move while you work. Scribe a line along the outside of the boards to mark for a cut line on the regular decking. Katwijk holds a carpenter's pencil sideways to produce a line that is a decking joint's thickness away.

4. Using a circular saw with a curve-cutting blade, cut along the lines. Work carefully, but not slowly; position yourself so you can cut long, smooth strokes.

5. Set the decking into the cutouts, and mark for cutting to length so that the joints split on a framing piece. Katwijk also applied curved pieces on top of this pergola.

THIS CURVED DESIGN is simpler to install. Because these boards run basically at right angles to the joists, there is no need to install a series of angled blocking pieces.

CLASSIC DESIGNS, INC.

Shawn Miller
Classic Designs, Inc.
Denver, Colorado
(303) 347-1212
www.deckdesigns.com

CLASSIC DESIGNS, INC.

Shawn Miller builds decks in the greater Denver area, where the weather stays dry and sunny most of the year. He runs a thriving business designing decks and running as many as six construction crews. He is also heavily involved with the North American Deck and Railing Association (NADRA), including a stint as its president.

The tastes of Coloradans vary widely. Miller builds quite a few earthy redwood and cedar decks, but lately composites have become the leading choice. Some of his decks ramble casually, while others present neatly outlined outdoor rooms. His building techniques often reflect the dryness of the climate.

SHAWN MILLER creates designs and selects materials that suit his clients' tastes and goals for their decks, right.

MOST DESIGNS consist of a series of outdoor rooms, below, and usually feature a distinctive woodworking detail or two.

DECKS IN DENVER can either ramble over the property, opposite bottom, or be more constrained and angular.

DESIGN CONSIDERATIONS

Miller prides himself in designing decks that feel comfortable and also have a richness of detail. This quality comes through often in subtle rather than flashy ways.

THE DECK AND THE HOUSE. Miller aims to build decks that fit with the house. He often focuses on a feature of the house—the siding, the shape of the back wall, a trim detail—and uses it as a design point for the deck.

He tries to "bring the inside outside" by making the deck feel like a part of the house rather than a totally different space. For instance, he takes care to position a deck to line up with the house's windows so it will not inhibit the view of the yard from the inside. He avoids stepping the deck down from the entry door so that the deck feels like another room of the house. If cooking and dining will be the main activities, he places the kitchen and dining areas close to the house; if lounging is what the owners will usually do, then he places a living area near the house. The slight extra convenience makes the deck more inviting.

The deck should be proportioned to the house: if too small, it will look like an afterthought; too big, and it will dwarf the house. In the

end, a deck should feel like another room of the house. When this is accomplished, people feel comfortable on the deck, even if they don't know just why.

Miller makes a conscious effort to see things through the customer's eyes. He talks to them casually for some time, coming to an understanding of their lifestyle. He then designs a deck to suit their practical needs.

IT'S IN THE DETAILS. A custom deck should have a custom look, and Miller's decks feature a wealth of details. On his wood decks, you'll find plenty of trim and exposed edges that are routered. These little extra touches allow his carpenters to show off their craftsmanship; the end result feels richer, even if the reason is not consciously recognized.

He rarely uses curved lines on his decks; somehow they just don't fit with the Southwest style. Instead, he makes extensive use of angles. His decking often runs at an angle and usually includes a "picture frame" border around the perimeter.

Most of his composite decks include at least one medallion or other deck design, often placed in the center of a dining or living area, where a table or fire pit may go. Medallions enrich a deck's appearance for a relatively small cost.

BRINGING THE INSIDE OUTSIDE with ample seating areas and built-ins, left, is a design goal.

CEDAR AND REDWOOD, right, are the materials of choice.

COMPOSITE DECKING, below, is becoming popular among Miller's clients.

CLASSIC DESIGNS, INC.

MATERIALS. Materials perform differently in a desert area than in less hot and dry regions. As is the case everywhere, composite and vinyl decking and railings perform well and are easy to maintain. Customers generally prefer composites in earth tones, such as browns, mahogany, and reds.

Surprisingly, tropical hardwoods such as ipé tend to cup and crack in his area, so Miller usually does not build with them. Pressure-treated lumber has these problems to an even greater extent.

Unlike in most of the country, redwood is readily available and practical in Miller's neck of the desert. Because the air is so dry most of the time, redwood with light-colored sapwood—which would rot quickly in other regions—lasts for decades. Redwood stands up to the heat and exhibits little cracking and cupping, especially if it is protected by a yearly application of sealer.

Cedar is nearly as durable and stable as redwood, and usually costs less. Again, Miller does not have to worry about getting the dark heart-wood; light-colored cedar is durable. Miller likes to mix his wood materials—for example, using redwood for the decking and rough-sawn cedar for the fascia and overhead.

COMPOSITE DECKING SYSTEMS, right, often include a composite railing system like this one. The support structure, however, is constructed from pressure-treated lumber.

LITTLE DETAILS, such as the fire pit shown at far right, are often included in Miller's decks. A favorite of his is a contrasting border on composite designs.

WHILE EXPENSIVE IN MOST OF THE COUNTRY, redwood, above, is easy to come by in the Denver area. The local climate makes it a good choice.

MILLER LIKES TO MIX wood tones in his designs. Note in the photo, right, the difference between the railing's top rail and the support posts. Also note the teal balusters.

MILLER'S TECHNIQUES

MASONRY TOUCHES

■ Miller surpasses code requirements and uses pressure-treated No. 1 Southern Yellow Pine for all his framing. In his area, framing lumber does not even need to be treated. Straight and stable framing lumber ensures that a deck will have a flat surface and crisp corners.

■ Miller builds his footings and posts differently from the other builders in the book. After temporarily supporting the framing, he hangs posts, with post anchors attached, and then pours concrete. The post ends up supported by a post anchor that rises above the ground.

■ He installs joists every 12 inches, even if 16-inch spacing will meet code. This makes for a stronger deck surface.

■ Many of his decks are built with redwood or cedar, materials that may not last in other areas but that do well in an arid climate, as long as they are kept well sealed.

■ Woodworking details abound in Miller's wood decks, adding richness to the design. Railings, skirts, and stairways also provide opportunities for trimwork. He makes sure his workers spend time with a router and/or sander, giving corners and edges a finished look.

■ Miller often incorporates masonry structures into or near his decks. (See, for example, the stone rail cap on page 222, and the granite countertop on page 210.)

■ Just about every one of his decks includes extensive lighting, which adds a "wow" factor when the sun goes down. Miller prides himself in his wiring plans and is always on the lookout for new fixtures that look great and provide interesting illumination patterns.

POST INSTALLATION

EXCEEDS CODE

WOODWORKING TOUCHES

MATERIAL SELECTION

SHELTERED or OPEN

THAT OLD SUN CAN BE FRIEND OR FOE, SO THIS DECK HAS TWO DIS-
TINCT AREAS THAT ALLOW YOU TO SIT IN SHELTERED COMFORT OR
TO ENJOY THE OPEN SKIES. THOUGH THE MATERIALS ARE ALL SYNTHETIC,
THE COLORS AND DESIGN GIVE IT THE FEEL OF NATURAL WOOD.

TWO SEPARATE LIVING AREAS was the design goal here. Miller placed a covered eating area, right, off of the kitchen. A lounging area complete with fire pit, below, is located two steps down from the eating area.

DESIGN CONSIDERATIONS

The old deck was just too small and too squarish. There was also a nice enough patio, but it was difficult to reach from the kitchen. The owners wanted a dining area right off the kitchen, a modest cooking area, and a spacious living area with a fire pit—all with easy access. The deck is designed to fit with the house's vinyl siding and trim, but to feel a bit more outdoorsy.

TWO LEVELS, TWO FUNCTIONS.
The kitchen door is about 6 feet above the yard, which slopes down away from the house. In this situation, building a deck at yard level would be possible only by stepping the levels down. The owners didn't want to do that; easy access to the deck from the house was more important than easy access from the yard. The lower level is only two steps down from the upper level, and an angled set of nine steps leads to the yard.

The upper level is about 15 feet square, enough room for a largish dining table and a pathway to the lower level. There is an angled cutout on one side, but not the usual angled cutout on the other side, which would produce a partial octagon. Instead, the deck points outward there, providing a nice space for a small serving table or for standing and looking outward. The pergola (overhead) follows these contours, defining the room and providing shade.

The lower level's living/lounging area is off center to allow traffic to flow from the kitchen and the garage door. A medallion decking feature is off center of the entire level, but it is in the center of the lounging area so that chairs can be comfortably arranged around a fire pit.

SHADE CONSIDERATIONS. The
white vinyl pergola above the dining area provides a good amount of shade for this south-facing deck. It's positioned to shelter people dining on the deck, but it also serves to cool the house. This part of the house contains large windows and a large, mostly glass, door. Sun beating on a wall and through the windows can really warm up the kitchen, and even a small amount of shade can make the house more comfortable and cut down on air-conditioning costs.

Because the sun shines on different parts of the deck depending on the time of day and the season, there is no area specially dedicated to the grill. The modest-size propane grill can be moved around to the lower or the upper level in order to find a shady spot.

MATERIALS. The composite decking and railing has a wood-grain finish and woody colors. The pergola is made of white powder-coated aluminum.

This makes the pergola blend closely with the house, while the deck itself is stylistically midway between the vinyl siding and the natural world.

Miller's years of deck-building experience have taught him to avoid some of the more well-known composite materials in favor of lesser-known decking and railing components that perform well in a hot climate. The owners are very pleased with how their deck resists fading and staining.

The deck's underside—its structural posts and beams—are on display. They could have been covered with skirting, but there was concern that so much lattice or vertical wood slats would have dominated the deck's appearance. As long as posts and beams are fairly straight and are kept nicely stained and finished, they add a nice rustic touch. The existing patio was left in place, making an ideal floor for a storage area.

PLAN VIEW

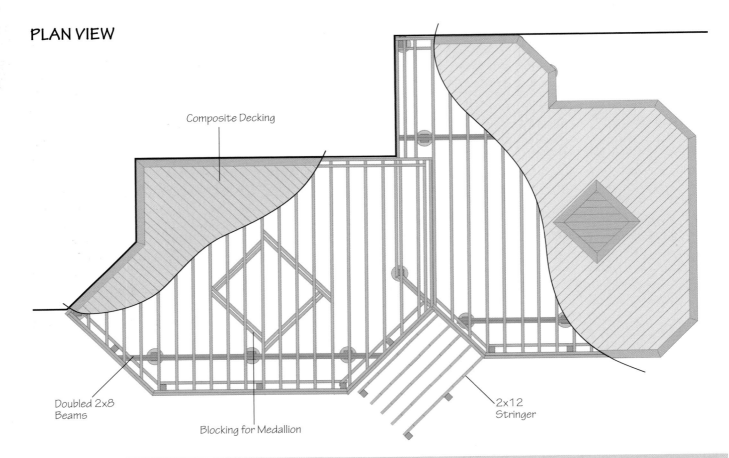

Composite Decking

Doubled 2x8 Beams

Blocking for Medallion

2x12 Stringer

MATERIALS USED FOR THIS DECK

Framing (all treated)	6x6 posts Doubled 2x8 beams 2x10 ledger and joists 2x12 stair stringers		2x4 composite top and bottom rails Metal pole balusters 1x6 composite rail cap
Decking and Fascia	1x6 composite decking ½-inch composite fascia board	Overhead (all aluminum)	3x8 beams 2x6 rafters 2x2 top pieces Caps and connectors supplied by manufacturer
Railing	4x4 treated posts Composite post sleeves and post caps		

CONSTRUCTION TECHNIQUES

CLASSIC DESIGNS, INC.

A mid-height deck like this calls for a few solid stepladders and good helpers, but no elaborate scaffolding. Though Miller's footings rise above the ground, he builds the framing with temporary supports and pours concrete later. You could instead install the footings first, but Miller's method makes layout mistakes less likely.

LEDGER. Lay out for lower and upper-level ledgers. In most areas of the country, you would typically position ledgers 2 inches or so below the door sills, so that once the decking is installed the deck will be an inch or so below the sill to keep out rain and leaves. In arid Colorado, Miller builds so the finished deck is just at the bottom of the sill. The lower deck is at a door that leads to the garage, and the upper deck is at the kitchen door. In a case like that, draw lines on the house, and make sure that the change in levels will equal one or two comfortable step rises; you may need to raise or lower one or both of the ledgers by an inch or so.

Install a ledger board, following your local codes to ensure that it is strong and will seal out water. On a house with wood or vinyl siding, Miller usually cuts out the siding, slips flashing up under the cut siding, and attaches a ledger using ¼-inch screws designed specifically for anchoring ledgers. Lay out for joists, spaced 16 or 12 inches apart, on the ledger.

If the deck is fairly high, you can dig the footing holes after framing. If it is lower than 4 feet or so, dig the footing holes before you build the framing.

FRAMING. Temporarily support the framing as you build it. Attach the outside and header joists, checking for level and supporting as you go. Lay out on the headers for inside joists. Install the inside joists, using joist hangers at the ledger and back-nailing at the headers.

Hang a beam under the joists. Cut the two 2x8 beam boards to length. Attach and temporarily support the first board; then attach the second board to the first using a grid of nails or screws.

If you will install 4x4 railing posts inside the framing (as on this deck), install them now. Cut them to the finished height, plus the width of the joists and the thickness of the decking. (The railing posts will be covered with composite sleeves and post caps after the decking is installed.) Three of the posts on this deck extend upward to support the overhead.

Double up the perimeter of the framing by attaching 2x10 "sister" boards all along the outside. Take care that the tops of the boards are perfectly flush; otherwise, the decking will not form a smooth surface. Drive a grid of nails or screws to laminate the boards. This will firm up the perimeter so that the railing posts will be rock-solid.

Elevation

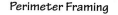

Aluminum Pergola

6x6 Posts

Perimeter Framing

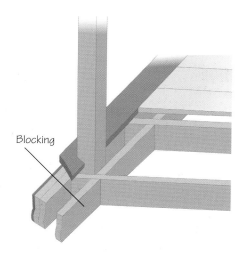

Blocking

MILLER USES POST ANCHORS like the one shown here. Drive nails or screws through the holes in the anchor to secure the post. Do the same for the post top at the other end of the post.

WITH THE FRAMING FIRMLY SUPPORTED determine the locations of the postholes. Dig the holes to the required depth. Hold the post over the hole.

To provide nailing surfaces for the picture-frame decking border as well as the regular decking, you could use the method shown on page 193. Here, a row of blocking pieces is installed 3½ inches away from doubled perimeter joists. The 3½-inch spacing allows the blocking pieces to enclose the 4x4 railing posts.

You will also want to provide framing for the medallions on both decks, using two rows of angled blocking pieces spaced about 2 inches apart. Measure and use a chalk line to mark the tops of the joists with the positions of the medallion's border. Install blocking pieces as needed so that the border and the decking pieces both inside and outside will be supported.

HANGING A STRUCTURAL POST. This method produces a post that rests on top of an aboveground footing. (Note that these photos show a flush beam; the same method holds for an under-joist beam.)

Once the beams are installed, check the framing for level and make any needed adjustments. Determine where you want the posts, and use a plumb bob (a chalk line works fine) to mark for the footing holes; then dig them. Miller generally digs holes about 36 inches deep. Your codes may call for deeper holes and may require that you install concrete tube forms.

Cut the post so its bottom will be 2 inches or so above grade. Attach a post top to one end and a post anchor to the other end.

Have a helper hold the post in position, centered over the hole with the post anchor extending into the hole. Or just hold it yourself using your foot. Drive nails or screws to attach the post. When you pour the concrete, mound it up an inch or so above grade. The post anchor will then hold the post about an inch above the concrete.

DECKING AND FASCIA. Install the regular decking first, allowing it to

ATTACH THE POST CAP to the beam by driving nails or screws into the beam. Follow the recommended nailing pattern to ensure firm attachment.

ANOTHER VIEW OF THE ATTACHED POST shows how the bottom of the anchor extends into the hole, which will be filled with concrete. The anchor holds the post aboveground.

run wild onto or past the doubled perimeter joists. You will need to make cutouts where the decking meets railing posts. Make a chalk-line cut, and install the decking border framing piece, as shown on page 193.

Cut pieces of fascia to fit between the railing posts, and install them tucked under the decking.

TO INSTALL THE BORDER you will need to add blocking along the perimeter of the framing. Miller installed blocking pieces 3½ in. away from the doubled perimeter joist.

STAIRS. For a medium-height set of stairs like this, start by determining the exact height at which they will end at the bottom. Build a concrete or paver landing pad at the bottom. Or build the forms for the concrete, and pour the concrete after you build the stairs. This landing pad has a concrete base topped with pavers.

Determine the total rise and run of the stairs, and then perform calculations so that all the steps will be the same individual rise (height) and run (depth). For a standard stairway like this, 6–7½-inch rises and 11–12 inch runs are typical and will feel familiar. Mark and cut a 2×12 to create a notched stringer. Be sure to take into account the thickness of the decking and the stair treads. In most cases, the bottom rise will be one tread's thickness shorter than the other rises.

Set the first stringer in place, against the deck joist and on the landing pad. Measure to make sure all the rises and runs will be equal, and check that the treads will be fairly close to level. Once you are satisfied, use the first stringer as a template to mark for the other stringers.

Attach the stringers by back-nailing through the joist; then attach strap hardware for extra strength.

RAILING. Cut post sleeves to height, and slip them over the 4x4 railing posts. Cut bottom and top composite rails to fit between the posts. With the rails set side by side on edge, lay out for the balusters. Drill holes, and slip the balusters into the holes to create a balustrade. Attach the balustrade to the posts using the hardware provided by the manufacturer. Cut and attach rail caps, and add post caps.

OVERHEAD. This overhead is made with aluminum components. The decorative rafter ends on one end are already formed; you need only cut the rafters to length at the other end. Cut and install the top pieces spaced to provide the desired amount of shade. Once all the pieces are installed, snap on the end caps provided by the manufacturer.

THESE STAIRS end at a concrete pad that is covered with concrete pavers.

MILLER MAKES EXTENSIVE USE of deck-framing hardware. Note the joist hangers shown here, as well as the straps to hold the stair stringers in place.

COMPOSITE POST SLEEVES fit over 4x4 railing posts. The balusters slip into holes drilled into the top and bottom rails.

CLASSIC DESIGNS, INC.

THE RAIL CAP FOR THE STAIRWAY is set on edge and has a routed groove on each side, making it a "graspable" rail.

THIS LOW-VOLTAGE LIGHT FIXTURE directs light both up and down.

THIS OVERHEAD is made from an aluminum kit. The support posts shown also support the railing. Once you have assembled all of the components, you simply snap on the decorative end pieces to finish the job.

A CHEERY RAMBLER

IN A FAIRLY SMALL SPACE, THIS DECK MANAGES TO FIT FOUR AREAS FOR
RELAXING AND EATING. NATURAL CEDAR AND COMPOSITE MATERIALS
ARE MIXED AND MATCHED TO MAKE FOR A DECK THAT FEELS ORGANIC
BUT IS EASY TO MAINTAIN. FANCIFUL STATUETTES AND OTHER DECO-
RATIVE TOUCHES MAKE THE DECK FEEL EVEN HOMIER.

JUST OUTSIDE THE BEDROOM, left, there is room for a small table and a few chairs.

AN EATING AREA off of the kitchen, right, rests in a small bump out of the deck. The table and chairs are sized so that they do not block the stairs.

DESIGN CONSIDERATIONS

The existing deck was a small rectangle that did not suit the owners' needs: it was not wide enough for a dining table, was not accessible from the bedroom door (which is to the left as you look at the deck from the yard), and had only one set of stairs, so you had to walk way around in order to get to the yard.

FOUR LIVING SPACES. The goal was to fit plenty of options into a modest-size area—and on a modest-size budget. The owners chose to place their grill on a nearby patio, which freed up deck space and kept cooking smoke out of people's eyes.

The upper deck has three defined areas. Just outside the kitchen door (on the right as you face the deck from the yard), an octagonal bump out creates an area large enough for a medium-size dining table, with a pathway between the table and the house. To the dining area's left is a narrower area, a good size for a few chairs. And all the way to the left, just outside a bedroom door, is what could be called a small lounge. The deck's angled contours and overhanging tree branches make this a nicely secluded spot.

A set of 4-foot-wide steps leads to a lower deck, that partially wraps around a hot tub, which is raised about 3 feet above the deck surface to make it easy to get in and out. There is no bench; instead, there is room for patio furniture that can be positioned as needed.

MIXED MATERIALS. The decking is a light beige composite, with a picture-frame border made of darker composite. The railing and fascia are primarily made of natural cedar, with a rail cap of the lighter-color composite decking. You might expect that butting natural and synthetic materials against each other would produce a discordant look, but actually, the cedar softens the composites and gives the whole deck a natural appearance.

With an arrangement like this, the wood parts must be painstakingly stained so that the stain does not spill or lap onto abutting composite parts.

Fortunately, this deck is well shaded by large trees so the deck is not subjected to intense sunlight, which is unusual in Colorado. That means that staining may only need to be done every other year.

COST-SAVING MOVES. The deck could easily have been larger, but Miller designed it to accomplish a lot in a small area. Decks are often priced by the square foot, so a smaller deck is almost always a less-expensive deck than a larger project. Cedar is less expensive than composites—and especially less expensive than composite rail components. So

constructing the rail with cedar saved a significant amount of money. Other cost cutters: the railing extends only partway around the hot tub; and there is no skirting under most of the upper deck.

DECORATING A DECK. Many people prefer a deck with a pristine, uncluttered appearance. However, even if the inside of your house is neat and tidy, feel free to experiment with a more jumbled appearance on the outside. Sculptures, figurines, personal artifacts, and flowerpots can be a mishmash of styles and still look great.

EXPRESS THE INNER YOU by how you choose to decorate and accessorize your deck. Flowers from your garden, left, quirky figurines, above, or even a piece of sculpture that speaks to you, below, are all possible additions.

CONSTRUCTION TECHNIQUES

CLASSIC DESIGNS, INC.

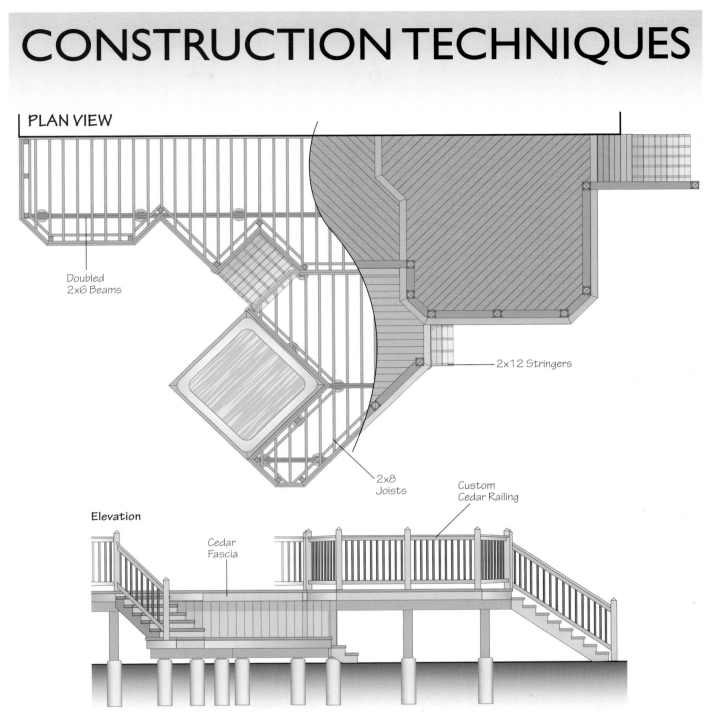

PLAN VIEW

Doubled
2x6 Beams

2x12 Stringers

2x8
Joists

Custom
Cedar Railing

Elevation

Cedar
Fascia

MATERIALS USED FOR THIS DECK

		Railing	4x4 cedar posts
Framing	Doubled 2x6 beams		2x4 cedar top and bottom rails
(all treated)	2x8 joists		⁵⁄₄x6 composite decking for cap rail
	2x12 stair stringers		Metal balusters
Decking	⁵⁄₄x6 composite decking		
and Fascia	Rough cedar 1x8 for fascia		

Because this deck has a good number of angles and turns, start with a detailed framing plan and follow it closely.

SUPPORT FOR A HOT TUB.
Consult with local codes and the manufacturer's literature to learn the approved and recommended way to support the hot tub. You may pour a reinforced concrete slab; install a gravel and sand bed; or build an extra-strong deck. You'll also need to run plumbing and electrical lines and provide access to the utilities. In this deck, the back of the hot tub is left open for easy access.

LEDGER AND FRAMING.
Install the ledger for the upper level, following local codes and providing flashing or using a standoff method in order to prevent water from wicking into the house. Draw layout lines on the ledger indicating where each joist will go.

Starting at one end of the ledger, cut the perimeter joists (the outside and header joists) and install them in order. See that the first board is at a right angle to the house. Check each board for level and temporarily support each as you go. At 45-degree turns, cut each board at a 22½-degree angle. Continually check that the boards are the correct distance from the house. For the header joists that are parallel with the house, check that they are the same distance from the house at each end.

Keep building until you have gone at least halfway around the upper deck; then start from the other end of the ledger and work toward the middle. Before you cut and install the final outside piece, double-check that the outside pieces are square to the house and that all the other angles are either 45 or 90 degrees.

Lay out and dig the footing holes. Use a string line to make sure the footings for each beam will be in a straight line.

Cut and install the joists to fit between the ledger and the perimeter joists. First install the joists that will butt against the perimeter joists that are parallel with the house. Make sure they will be at right angles to the ledger. Then, measuring off those joists, install the other joists, which will be cut at 45 degrees at the outer ends. As you work, continually check that the joists are parallel with and the correct distance from each other.

Temporarily support the beam under the joists. You may build the two-part beam first, or you may install one of the 2x6s to the underside of the joists, then add the other. Cut the structural posts so their bottoms will be 2 inches or so above grade; add a post anchor at the bottom and a post top at the top; and attach the post so it hangs over the hole. (See page 194.)

Once the upper deck framing is finished, do the same for the lower deck. Install the framing an inch or two away from the hot tub; the decking will overhang the framing.

Cut and attach the railing posts to the inside of the perimeter joists. To provide nailing surface for the perimeter decking frame and the regular joists, double up the perimeter joists, and add a row of blocking 3½ inches from the perimeter. This will allow you to sandwich the railing posts. (See page 193.)

DECKING AND FASCIA.
Install a row of cedar picture-frame decking along the house. Then install the regular decking, allowing it to run wild onto or past the doubled perimeter joists. You will need to make cutouts where the decking meets railing posts. Make a chalk-line cut, and install the decking border framing piece.

Cut pieces of fascia to fit between the railing posts, and install them tucked under the decking.

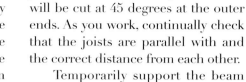

SPAS USUALLY REQUIRE EXTRA SUPPORT. You will need to pour a concrete pad or a firm gravel base. Check with the spa manufacturer for specific recommendations. You will also need to supply access to plumbing and electrical lines.

CUTTING A DECORATIVE POST TOP

YOU COULD PURCHASE DECORATIVE POST CAPS, which simply attach to the top of a straight-cut post. Or create your own custom design by cutting the top yourself.

1. Two in. or so down from the top of the post, use a square to draw a cut line all around the post.

2. Set a power miter saw to cut at 45 deg., and cut along all four lines, to create a point. You can do this with a circular saw, as long as you keep the saw's baseplate perfectly flat against the post as you work.

3. Set the saw to cut at 90 deg., and cut the top off of the point.

4. Two in. or so below the cuts, draw lines for the groove, 1 in. apart, all around the post.

5. Adjust a circular saw to cut to a depth of ½ in.

6. Cut just to the inside of the lines. Then make a series of closely spaced cuts inside the groove.

7. Use a sharp chisel to clean out the grooves.

CLASSIC DESIGNS, INC.

A REDWOOD BEAUTY

THIS DECK IS LARGE ENOUGH TO ACCOMMODATE A GOOD-SIZE PARTY, YET IT FEELS COZY BECAUSE OF ITS RAMBLING SHAPE AND THE WARMTH OF THE STAINED REDWOOD.

HERE, OLD DECKING has been sanded and stained. Though it has some cracks, it retains all of its charm.

DESIGN CONSIDERATIONS

Much of the deck's current top level already existed in the form of a rectangular deck that had only one stairway to the rear. Where the current lower deck is now, there was a ground-level patio. The owners liked the look of redwood, but they wanted more space. Also, they had to walk way around and down to reach the patio, which was inconvenient. The current two-level deck maintains the look of redwood and makes it easy to move between levels.

BRICK AND WOOD. Against the backdrop of a brick or stone wall, natural stained wood usually looks better than composite materials. (White painted wood would also look good, but a painted deck surface is not practical.) Here, the wood is sealed with a light tan-colored stain, which contrasts nicely with the red bricks. A reddish stain would also look good and would blend more than it would contrast.

There was originally a third brick pillar, in the middle between the two pillars that remain. It blocked the view from the house, so it was removed.

BUILDING IN PHASES. If your funds don't match your deck dreams, you don't have to live with no deck or a deck you dislike. In many cases, it is possible to build some of what you want now, leaving room for the things you will add later.

The deck you are looking at is actually phase two of a three- or four-phase overall plan. Phase two has expanded on the old, small deck to create more space and some interesting angles. In the future, the owners plan to add an outdoor kitchen (with a counter, a built-in grill, and other cooking accessories)

where the grill now stands. They also plan to install a large built-in fire pit on the lower level; for the moment, a portable fire pit serves their purposes.

THE PLAN. Stepping out of the house, there is an area to the right with enough space for a couple of lounge chairs and a small table. On the other side, a dining area is positioned near the railing, and a cooking space is a few feet away. The deck can also be accessed via a small stairway at the rear.

Moving down a 5-foot-wide stairway, you enter a large open deck area. Only one of the corners is angled. There are no built-in benches or planters; furniture can be moved around to suit the needs of a large gathering or a small group huddled around a fire pit.

A PARTICULARLY BEAUTIFUL piece of redwood is put on display when used as the stairway's rail cap.

CONSTRUCTION TECHNIQUES

PLAN VIEW

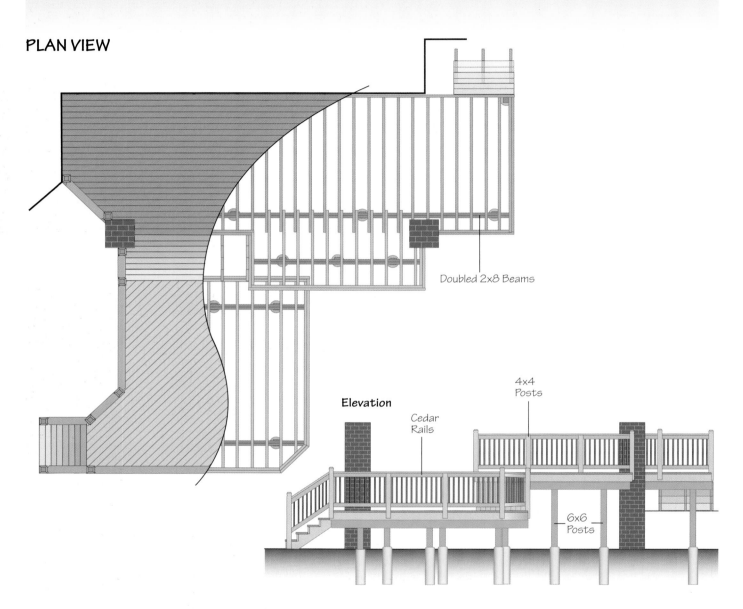

Doubled 2x8 Beams

Elevation

Cedar Rails

4x4 Posts

6x6 Posts

MATERIALS USED FOR THIS DECK

Framing (all treated)	6x6 posts Doubled 2x8 beams 2x8 ledger and joists 2x12 stair stringers	Railing
Decking and Fascia	2x6 redwood decking 1x8 rough-cut cedar fascia	Skirting levels

Railing	4x4 cedar posts 2x4 cedar top and bottom rails Metal balusters 2x6 cedar rail cap
Skirting levels	2x4 cedar for skirting between upper and lower levels ¾-in. cedar lattice panels for skirting under lower level

The deck is built like most others: temporarily support the joists; add the beams under the joists; hang the posts; then pour the concrete. The upper level is an extension of the old deck, which introduces a few new techniques.

FRAMING. When extending a deck as was done with the upper level here, remove any fascia, skirting, and other obstacles. If possible keep existing posts, beams, and footings. You may choose to remove a header or outside joist, then run new joists so they overlap alongside the existing joists by two feet or more, as we show here. Or you could leave the header or outside joist, and add new joists using joist hangers.

The extended framing for the upper level has an extra beam, which might not have been necessary had all the framing been built at once. When supporting the joists and hanging the beam and posts, raise the front edge of the new framing up slightly—3/8 inch or so—because it will settle slightly.

Plan the height of the lower level so the stairs leading down to it will have consistent rises of 7 inches (or if you prefer, 6 or 7½ inches).

DECKING AND FASCIA. Where decking is extended along its length, you may need to remove or cut back some existing boards so you can "weave in" the new boards; if you just add the new boards to the ends of the old, the resulting straight line of butt joints will be unattractive.

Hidden fasteners can be used to install redwood decking, but in this case the existing decking had exposed screwheads, so the rest of the deck follows suit. The screwheads are definitely visible, so take care to drive them in fairly straight rows. As you install the decking, start by driving only as many screws as needed to keep them straight. Once a decking section is complete, snap chalk lines

THE BRICK PILLAR was part of the original deck design. The owners left two in place but removed a third because it blocked the view.

and drive screws along them.

Let the decking boards run wild; then mark with a chalk line; and cut so they overhang the joists by 2 inches or so. Cut pieces of 1x8 fascia to fit, and tuck them under the decking.

STAIRS. You can build the stairs either before or after laying the decking. For the wide stairs that span between the deck levels, lay out for and cut four or five notched stringers. Provide a solid fastening surface to attach the top of the stringers, and use straps or other hardware in addition to backnailing them. Use two decking boards for the treads, and rip-cut pieces of 1x8 for the risers.

RAILING WITH CORNER POSTS. Most railings in this book do not have posts at the exact outside corners; instead, Miller usually places posts near the corners on each side. A corner-post railing has an old-fashioned appeal.

Some of these posts have decorative tops that rise above the rail cap; others rise only to the underside of the rail cap. For the taller posts, cut and rout a decorative post top. (See

RAILING POSTS must be notched to fit around the framing on this deck. Check code requirements in your area before notching posts. Because the original deck had exposed fasteners, the owners opted to follow suit on the new section.

Notched Rail Posts

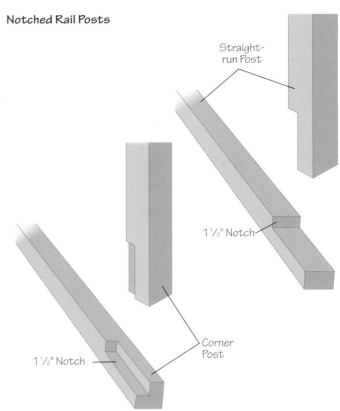

Straight-run Post

1½" Notch

1½" Notch

Corner Post

THESE POSTS ARE NOTCHED and attached to the outside of the fascia. Ledger screws are used rather than the more traditional ½-inch lag screws with washers. The ledger screws are just as strong, and less visually obtrusive.

TO KEEP GATES FROM SAGGING IN THE FUTURE, install a diagonal turnbuckle extension rod to the inside face of the gate. Miller used a biscuit joiner to secure the pieces of the frame to one another.

"Cutting a Decorative Post Top" page 203.) Cut the posts to length.

One drawback of using corner posts is that you will need to notch all posts at the bottom. The notch allows the post to wraparound the corner. Some local codes do not allow notched posts; if that is the case in your area, you cannot install corner posts. To notch most of the posts, mark for a cutout that is 1½ inches deep and 6 or 7 inches long. Cut with a circular saw; then use a handsaw or reciprocating saw to finish the cut.

Notching a corner post is a bit more complicated. Cut as much as you can with a circular saw. Then use a chisel to remove the rest.

Build balustrades to fit between the posts. Cut 2x4 top and bottom rails to fit; then lay out for and drill holes for evenly spaced balusters. Assemble the balustrades; attach them by drilling angled pilot holes and driving screws into the posts. Cut the cap rail, and cut little corner details at the ends. Attach to the top of the top rail.

GATE. To build this gate, cut 2x4s at 45-degree miters to make a frame that is ⅜ inch narrower than the opening between the posts. Hold the long pieces side by side, and mark for evenly spaced metal balusters. Drill holes, and assemble the balusters with the 2x4s. Position the side 2x4s, and check for square and correct size. Working on a flat surface, use a biscuit joiner and long clamps to join the pieces together. (See "Biscuit Joinery," on page 64 for tips on using a biscuit joiner.) Check the frame for square as you work. To reinforce the joints, drill pilot holes, and drive 3-inch screws into the joints.

Sand the wood edges so they are slightly rounded. Attach strap hinges to the gate. Temporarily support the gate as you screw the hinges to the post. Add the latch hardware. To keep the gate from going out of square in years ahead, add a turnbuckle tension

THE LATTICE PANELS are attached directly to the support beam. This places the lattice a foot or so inside the perimeter joists, giving the appearance of a floating deck.

rod assembly, which can be tightened or loosened as needed.

SKIRTING. To provide a nailing surface for the skirting, use nailing plates to add a simple framework. Cut redwood lattice panels to fit, and attach with nails. Cover the joints with redwood 1x4s.

FINISHING TOUCHES. Wood decking and railing caps are prone to splinter, so for safety's sake and to provide a nice little finish detail, round off the sharp edges. Use a router with a roundover bit, or you can use just a hand sander for the job. Apply stain and sealer immediately, before the deck gets dirty.

MOST OF THIS UPPER DECK SURFACE is an older deck; only portions are new. After careful sanding and staining, the difference in appearance is barely noticeable.

BARBECUE COUNTER

OUTDOOR KITCHENS CONTINUE TO GROW IN POPULARITY, AND FOR GOOD REASON. COOKING IS TRANSFORMED FROM A CHORE INTO A CONVIVIAL JOY WHEN DONE OUTDOORS. PEOPLE ALL AROUND THE COUNTRY REPORT THAT ONCE THEY INSTALL AN OUTDOOR COOKING CENTER, THEY START SPENDING MUCH MORE TIME ON THEIR DECK WITH FAMILY AND FRIENDS.

PURCHASE COMPONENTS, such as drawer units, above, online or from a grill specialty store.

GRANITE, right, makes a great countertop material Other choices include tile, concrete, or other natural stone.

CLASSIC DESIGNS, INC.

CHOOSING AMENITIES

At a barbecue specialty store or online you can find a wide range of outdoor kitchen components. The counter shown here houses a large propane grill, a propane stove-top burner, a set of drawers, and two doors for access to storage space. Also available: sinks with running water, refrigerators, warming trays, sound systems, TVs—the listing goes on and on. You can even add a wood-fired pizza oven or a fireplace.

BUILDING OPTIONS

Many outdoor kitchen counters are made of very heavy concrete block, plus stone or tile; these must rest on a concrete footing, and so are suitable for a patio but not a deck. You can also buy a factory-made counter equipped with a grill, doors, and other amenities. But many people prefer to custom build a counter that suits their deck style.

The counter shown here, made with wood or metal studs, is certainly heavy enough to stay in place (the granite top assures that), but is not nearly as heavy as a masonry counter. This counter is finished with tongue-and-groove cedar, trimmed with cedar 1-byes. The top is a granite slab, ordered cut to fit by a granite company. Another popular option: cover the sides with concrete backer board, then apply stone or ceramic tiles to the backer board. The top can be made of wood that is well sealed, tiles, natural stone, or cast concrete.

Start by measuring your components and consulting manufacturer's literature to be sure everything will fit in the openings. As you plan and build the framing, take into account the thickness of the finish materials.

Construct a 2x4 frame (you could also use metal studs). Fasten the joints using decking screws. At the bottom, you may choose to build a floor of treated plywood, but the deck itself can serve as a floor; the gaps between decking boards let any collected water seep through. To firm up the counter's top, cut and attach a piece of ¾-inch plywood.

Run utility lines as needed. You may need an electrical line for a receptacle, plumbing supply lines for running water, and a plumbing drain line for a sink. If you will be using natural gas, run a gas line, as well. Hook up a propane tank later.

Cut and attach siding pieces, checking as you go to make sure the grill and doors will fit. Install the doors and the drawer unit. Order a piece of granite. The granite company will likely come out and measure. When you attach the grill and any other items that rest on top, caulk the flanges well to prevent rainwater from seeping below.

Framing Detail

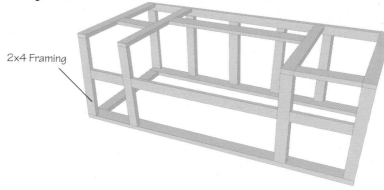

2x4 Framing

A TWO-LEVEL DECK

THIS DECK WAS DESIGNED TO FLOW INTO THE YARD, AND IT DOES SO
BEAUTIFULLY. IT FEATURES TWO COMFY, RELAXING AREAS SNUGGED UP
AGAINST THE HOUSE AND SHELTERED BY PERGOLAS OVERHEAD. A BIT
FARTHER OUT IS A DINING AREA. A LOWER LEVEL JUTS OUT INTO THE
YARD LIKE THE PROW OF A SHIP AND IS ANCHORED BY A STUNNING
BENCH/PLANTER COMBO. A LARGE STORAGE BOX HELPS TO KEEP
THINGS ORGANIZED.

A SEATING AREA projects into the yard, left. The area is enclosed with built-in benches and planters. A center medallion serves to anchor the design.

BUILT-IN STORAGE, below, keeps sports equipment handy and well organized.

DESIGN CONSIDERATIONS

As so often happens, the owners were tired of a small, rectangular deck that could not accommodate their needs and did nothing for their sense of style. Miller designed a multiangle deck that gave them room to stretch out and enjoy themselves.

THE ROOMS. This backyard has some large trees that by supper time shade the entire deck. The pergolas provide shade for earlier hours of the day.

Walking out the kitchen door (to the right and rear in the photo opposite), you enter an area just wide enough for a set of lounge chairs on one side, a modest grill on the other, and a clear pathway between. This area is sheltered by a pergola; for a lunch on a sunny day, the dining table can be moved here.

The dining area is more or less in the middle of the upper deck level. To the left, against the house, is an area made specifically with a hammock in mind, a spot that is just right for an afternoon siesta in dappled sun. There is ample room for a path to the mudroom door located nearby.

In front, a lower level, shaped almost like an arrowhead, offers inviting seating possibilities with a built-in bench that follows its contours. Planters with colorful flowers flank either side of the bench, and a medallion in the middle marks the spot for a fire pit or table.

MATERIALS. All the surfaces are covered with composite lumber. When wet, this material seems to shine and almost glow. When dry, it recedes in appearance. An experienced builder can recommend materials that will endure and remain good-looking. The two colors—brown and tan—make the deck feel natural and colorful at the same time.

THE OVERHEADS. Many overheads feature exposed rafter and beam ends, often cut in fanciful shapes, and top pieces that jut out decoratively. Here, the ends are boxed in with wide pieces of composite fascia board. This minimizes the visual impact of the overheads—which is in keeping with

a house that does not have a lot of decoration.

Because the deck is low, the two railings are not required by code, but they add a nice ornamental touch and help enclose the two lounging areas. Without them, the pergola posts would seem stranded.

PLANTER/BENCH AND STORAGE. Most people sitting around the fire prefer to sit on Adirondack chairs rather than the built-in bench, but the bench is handy when there are more than a few people. Because it is simple and backless, it does not inhibit the view of the yard.

CONSTRUCTION TECHNIQUES

PLAN VIEW

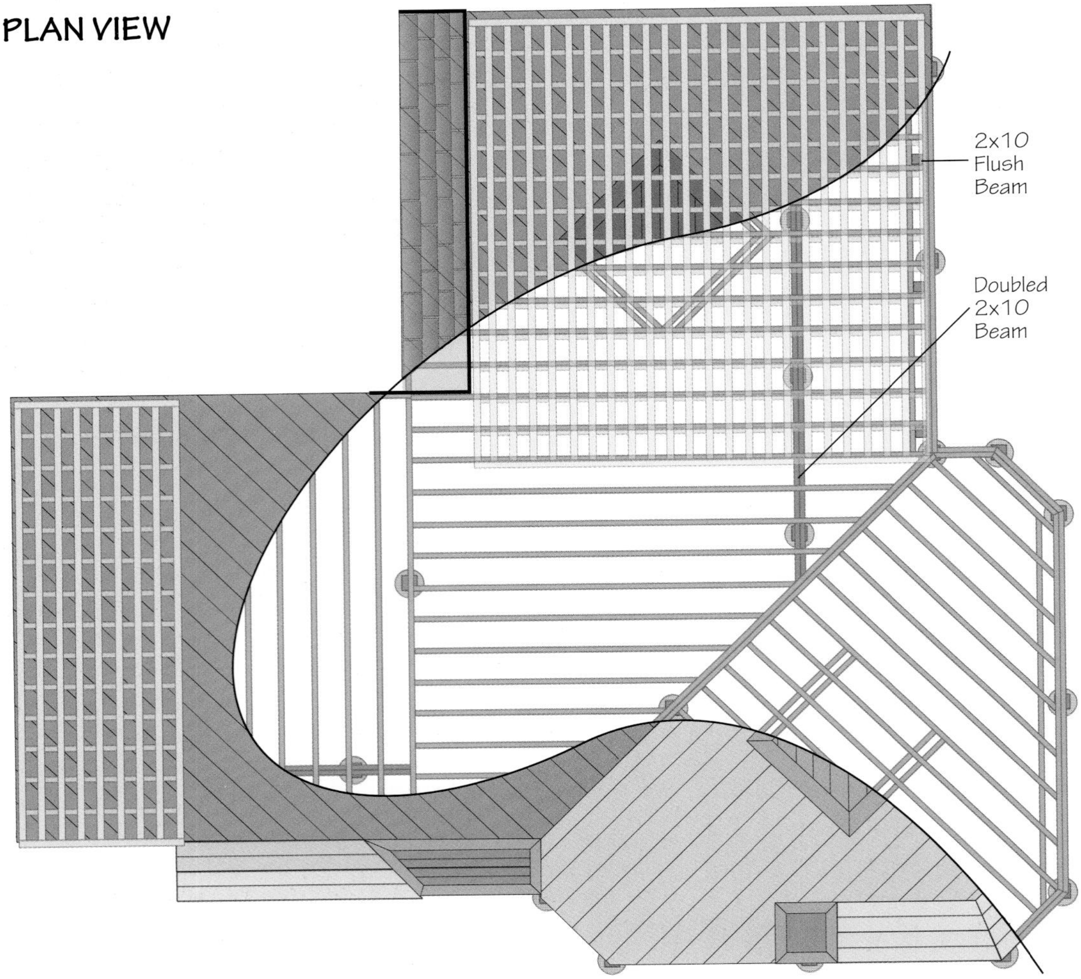

Under-Joist Beam

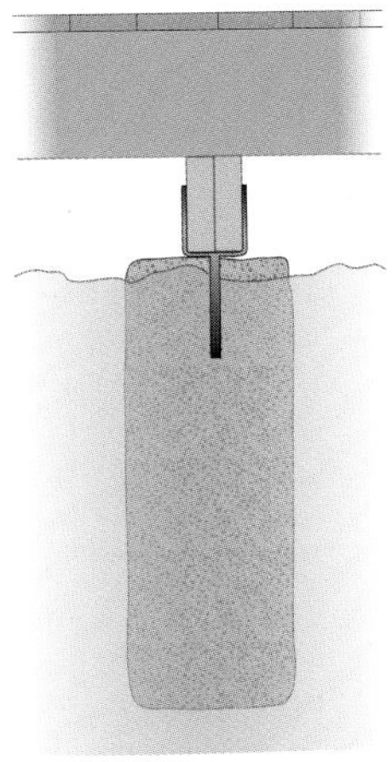

2x10
Flush
Beam

Doubled
2x10
Beam

Flush Beam

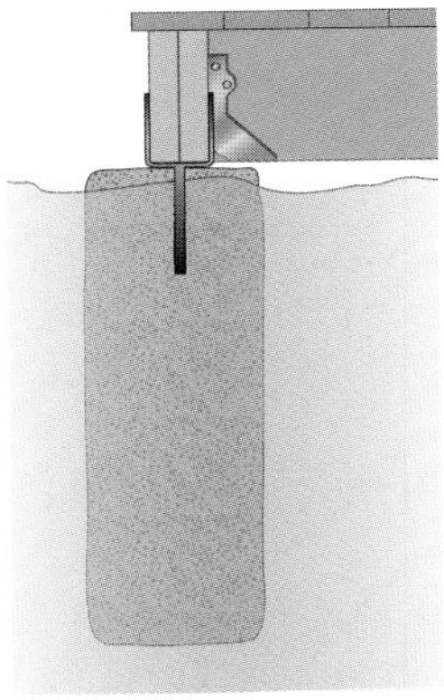

Framing (all treated)	Doubled 2x6 beams 2x8 ledger and joists	Overhead	Treated 2x10 flush beams Treated 2x6 rafters Composite 1x6 (ripped to 1x3s) for top pieces Composite fascia board
Decking and Fascia	⁵⁄₄x6 composite decking Composite fascia board		
Railing	Treated 4x4 posts (also used for overhead) Composite post sleeves Composite top and bottom rails Metal balusters Composite decking for rail cap	Bench/Planter	Treated 4x4 posts Composite post sleeves Treated 2x4 for framing Treated plywood inside planter Composite decking
		Storage Box	Treated 2x4 framing Treated plywood Composite decking

ALTHOUGH NOT REQUIRED BY CODE, this railing with its curved metal balusters adds a decorative touch to this part of the deck.

BECAUSE THE JOINT BETWEEN DECKING AND HOUSE IS HIGHLY VISIBLE, take the time to install it nice and tight.

A very low deck like this offers unique construction challenges. There are no structural posts. The upper level has three under-joists beams, which rest directly on footings. The lower level has flush beams (meaning that they are on the same plane as the joists, which join to them via joist hangers), and these too rest directly on footings.

Note: the angled under-joist beam at the front of the upper level also acts as a flush beam for the lower deck: it both supports the joists above, and it has joists tied into it with joist hangers.

BUILDING OPTIONS. One possible method: first carefully lay out for and dig footing holes; then use a transit level to help pour the footings (with embedded post anchors) at the correct heights. Once the concrete has set, install the beams, then the joists. However, it's easy to make layout and pouring mistakes that way. So Miller builds the joist framing on temporary supports, and then he hangs the beams and pours the concrete.

EXCAVATION. Use a transit level, water level, or carpenter's level atop a straight board to roughly determine whether you need to excavate away any high spots. All the boards should be at least 2 or 3 inches away from the ground.

FRAMING THE UPPER LEVEL. Attach the ledger, following local codes to ensure it is strong and will keep water away from the house.

Lay out for and dig the footing holes for the upper level. (You may choose to do this later, after part of the joist framing is completed, but the framing may get in the way of the digging.) Note that in addition to the footings for the under-joist beams there are two footings for the perimeter framing. Set tube forms in the holes; later, you will raise them all up to the same height.

Construct the joist framing on temporary supports. Once you are certain it is level, hang beams under the joists, directly above the footing holes. Attach a metal beam anchor (made to attach a beam to a concrete footing) to the bottom of the beams at

each footing hole, hanging down into the center of the hole. Raise each tube form to the correct height, so it will support the beam while holding it up slightly. Tack scrap boards against the forms to hold them temporarily in position, and pour the concrete. Wait for the concrete to set before installing the decking.

FRAMING THE LOWER LEVEL. Lay out for and dig the footing holes, which run around the perimeter of the framing. Set tube forms into the holes. Construct the joist framing on temporary supports. Use the upper level's angled beam like a ledger, attaching joists to it via joist hangers. Double up the perimeter joists to create flush beams. Hang beam anchors from the flush beams into the centers of the footing holes. Raise the tube forms to the correct height, and pour the concrete.

DECKING. Install the 4x4 posts for the railing and the overheads. Add rows of blocking to support the decking border. (See "Installing a Border," page 219.)

A CONTRASTING BORDER, above, is a nice design touch when added to a composite deck. This material has a wood-grain appearance.

A PERGOLA, below, provides shade to part of the deck. A matching structure is on the other side of the deck. In this design, the cross pieces are boxed in with composite material.

OVERHEAD AND RAILING. Slip composite post sleeves, as well as post bottom trim, over the railing and overhead posts. Use angled braces to temporarily support the overhead posts so that they stay plumb and stable as you work. Build the overhead's perimeter frame using the 2x12 resting atop the posts. At several points, tie the frame to the house using spacer blocks and screws to make the overhead stable. Lay out for and attach the rafters, spaced 16 inches apart. For the top pieces, rip-cut decking boards in half to make 1x3s. Lay out for top pieces that are evenly spaced, and attach them to the top of the rafters. Wrap the outside frame with fascia board.

For the railing, cut and attach composite 2x4 top and bottom rails to the posts, and install evenly spaced metal balusters.

PLANTER AND BENCH. Construct 2x4 frames for the planters, and line the bottoms and sides with treated plywood. Drill a series of ⅜-inch holes in the plywood bottom for drainage. Cover the sides and top with decking pieces to fit. Once constructed, place the planters where they will go on the deck.

Add a 2x4 cleat to the sides of the planters to support the seat pieces. Construct a simple frame using 4x4 posts, covered with composite post sleeves, and 2x4s. Cover with composite decking.

Build the storage box in the same way, with a 2x4 frame and plywood lining. Cover the sides with decking boards, and top with mitered boards. Build the box's hatch door out of 2x4s and composite decking material, and add two handles. Interior cleats support the hatch.

THE PLANTER AND BENCH COMBINATION serves a few purposes. It encloses the lounging area, provides additional seating, and adds color to the design. Cleats attached to the planter support the bench.

ATTACHING COMPOSITE DECKING

IF YOU WILL ATTACH COMPOSITE DECKING WITH SCREWS, there are two basic options—you can use small-headed decking screws or self-tapping screws. Both securely attach the decking; whichever you select is a matter of personal choice.

POUNDING MUSHROOMS. Drive small-headed composite decking screws so they sink ⅛ to ¼ in. beneath the surface (1). Squeeze with your fingers and push the little shavings down into the resulting hole (2). Then pound with a hammer to produce a slight "mushroom" shape (3). In time, the mushroom will smooth out and be only slightly visible.

SELF-TAPPING SCREWS. Some composite decking screws are "self-tapping," meaning that they cut out a neat hole for the fastener head (4). You can buy these screws in colors to match the decking.

DRESSING UP COMPOSITE DECKING

BECAUSE COMPOSITE DECKING IS A CONSISTENT COLOR, IT CAN BE USED TO MAKE ATTRACTIVE GEOMETRIC PATTERNS. IN FACT, MOST COMPOSITE DECKS HAVE AT LEAST TWO COLORS. A MONOTONE DECK WILL LOOK BLAND UNLESS THERE ARE OTHER DECORATIVE FEATURES.

DECKING BORDERS

A border, also called a picture frame, winds around all or part of a deck's perimeter. You may also install a border in the middle of a decking area to define two or more areas or simply to make an attractive pattern.

Where the deck meets the house, you may decide to install the border piece first, then the regular decking.

Everywhere else, run the regular decking so it runs past where the border will go; then cut an outline for the border pieces.

Decide how far you want the border to overhang the framing, if at all. A slight overhang will produce a shadow. In the example on these pages, the decking does not overhang; the fascia board will come up flush to the deck surface, as you can see in photo 6 below.

INSTALLING A BORDER

A DECKING BORDER provides a design flourish and a touch of color that is absent from most decks.

1. At each corner, look between decking boards to see the outside joist; measure over; and mark with a pencil. Mark for lines running in both directions.

2. Snap chalk lines running from mark to mark.

3. Adjust a circular saw's depth so it cuts just through the decking. If you are confident of your skills, cut along the lines freehand. Otherwise, first tack a straight board on the decking to use as a guide.

4. Use a chisel to finish the cuts at corners.

5. Cut all the lines, and remove the boards. Check that there will be adequate nailing surface for the border, and that none of the regular decking boards is unsupported at its end. Add blocking pieces if needed.

6. Where possible, hold the border pieces in place and mark, rather than using a tape measure. Use 45-deg. miters at 90-deg. corners, and 22½-deg. miters at 45-deg. corners. Check the joints for tight fits as you go; you may need to slightly adjust the angle from time to time. Drive screws into a board only when you are certain that the next piece will fit tightly.

INSTALLING A MEDALLION

A MEDALLION helps to make a deck an orderly place. It is often placed in the center of a deck area or at the planned location of a table or fire pit.

1. The framing must support the medallion's frame, its interior boards, and the ends of the regular decking boards surrounding the medallion. In the example shown, a double row of blocking is used on two sides, and only a single row is needed for the other two sides. In the following steps, you will see blocking that provides a wide fastening surface.

2. Install regular decking over the area where the medallion will be. Cut the medallion's frame pieces at 45-deg. miters. Carefully position the frame pieces on top of the deck. Measure to make sure they are correctly placed, and look between the decking boards to make sure you will have nailing surfaces below.

3. Once you are certain the frame is correctly placed and perfectly square, use a pencil to scribe a line around it. Take care not to move the frame pieces.

4. Adjust a circular saw's depth to cut just through the decking. Cut along the lines, stopping when you reach a corner.

5. Remove the cut boards. Use a hammer and chisel to complete and clean up the cuts at the corners.

6. Set the frame pieces in the opening, and check that the gap between the frame pieces and the decking is consistent all around.

7. Measure from corner to corner, and cut a decking board to fit. Make 45-deg. cuts that meet in the middle of the board on each side. Set the center board into the frame.

8. Drive screws to fasten the frame and the middle piece. To measure for the remaining pieces, hold one piece next to the previous one and mark, rather than using a tape measure. Set the boards in place, and drive screws to fasten.

A COMPOSITE MEDALLION helps to anchor an activity area on a deck, much as an area rug does when placed on a wood floor. Two possibilities are shown above and right. You can also simply cluster chairs around a medallion for a designated seating area. Miller uses contrasting composite decking for his medallions, but you can also take the same idea when building a wood deck and inlay ceramic or stone tile.

WOOD AND STONE VERANDA

HERE'S A SMALL DECK WITH SUPERSIZED CHARACTER. A WIDE RAILING
WITH A STONE SHELF ENCLOSES THE DECK, AND A STUNNING PERGOLA
SHADES IT.

THE ORIGINAL DECK was in good shape, so the owners chose to leave it in place but add a pergola and a limestone-capped railing.

DESIGN CONSIDERATIONS

The old rectangular redwood deck already existed, and the owners wanted Miller to spruce it up rather than rebuild it. They were happy with the size and simple shape; they just wanted a nice place to sit, relax, and enjoy the outdoors—cooking and dining are done on a patio off to the side.

A MIX OF MATERIALS. This deck proves that when it comes to outdoor structures, not everything needs to match. Here we have a green siding to match the house; nearly white limestone topping the railing; rough older redwood decking; and an overhead of lightly stained cedar. Add a few flowers (which, no matter the color, seem to go with anything), and the whole ensemble sings in harmony.

THE VIEW FROM THE DECK. The rectangular deck leaves room for lounge chairs and a pathway in front of them. The old decking could have been replaced, or sanded and refinished, but the owners were happy with the rustic appearance.

THE RAILING AND SHELF. Here's an unusual and pretty touch: the railing is 12 inches wide, with a 16-inch-wide limestone cap. The limestone is rough enough to provide plenty of rustic character but level enough so pots, figurines, and drinks set on it are sufficiently stable for all practical purposes.

Limestone is a semiporous rock, meaning that it can be cleaned of dirt and grime, but it can also be stained if red wine is spilled on it. Applying a simple masonry sealer will make it easy to clean.

THE OVERHEAD. Rough cedar of a fairly consistent color makes for an overhead that is woodsy without feeling too rustic. High-quality lumber must be used to avoid cracks and warping.

The rafters have a classic ogee shape where they protrude outward. On top, "self-spaced" 1x3s provide ample shade.

A CEDAR PERGOLA provides plenty of shade for the deck. It is lightly stained to help it blend in with the redwood deck.

CONSTRUCTION TECHNIQUES

PLAN VIEW

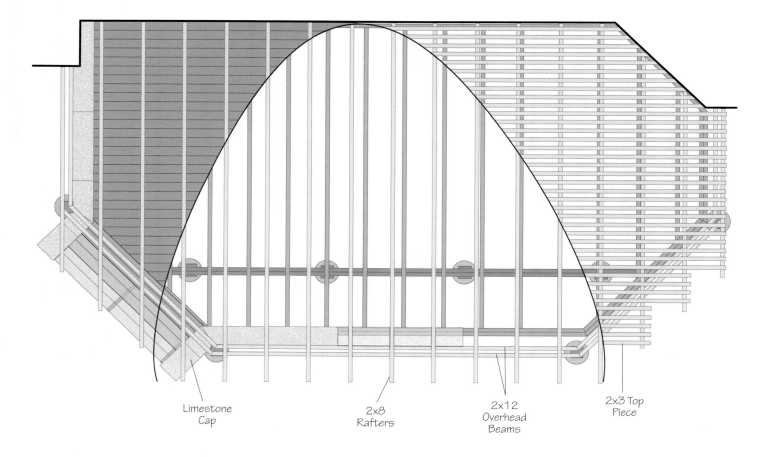

Limestone
Cap

2x8
Rafters

2x12
Overhead
Beams

2x3 Top
Piece

MATERIALS USED FOR THIS DECK

Framing (all treated)	4x4 posts Doubled 2x8 beams 2x8 ledger and joists 2x12 stair stringers	Railing	Treated 2x8 framing Horizontal siding for front and back 16-in.-wide limestone for cap
Decking	2x6 redwood decking	Overhead (all cedar)	6x6 posts 2x12 beams 2x8 rafters 2x3 top pieces

RAILING/LEDGE. To build the railing, construct a short stud wall, using 2x8s rather than 2x4s. Cover the sides with siding that comes up flush to the top of the framing.

Order pieces of limestone of the desired width. Cut the limestone to length using a rented masonry cutoff saw. Or you can cut using a grinder equipped with a masonry blade. To make the cuts straight, clamp a scrap board against the cut line and cut with the blade against the board.

Set the pieces in a dry run, to make sure they fit. You may choose to have ⅜-inch-wide joints between the pieces, or butt them tightly together. Remove and install one piece at a time. Consult with your inspector or a local builder for the best type of adhesive to use in your area; epoxy or polyurethane adhesives work better than standard construction adhesive. Use a caulk gun to make squiggles, or apply with a notched trowel, to both the top of the framing and the underside of the stone, and set the stone in place. Once all the stones are placed, apply grout to the joints.

OVERHEAD. This is a classic overhead with "flying" rafters resting atop beams and supporting evenly spaced

THE PERGOLA is supported by 6x6 beams. You can arrange the top cross pieces to provide the desired amount of shade.

top pieces. Start by pouring footings for the bottoms of the posts. The posts do not have to sink into the ground; they will gain lateral support by being tied to the railing. Insert a J bolt into each footing so that you can attach an adjustable post anchor.

Cut the posts to height. At their tops, cut notches 1½ inches deep and the width of the 2x12 beam pieces on either side. (The angled beam pieces will not be set into notches.) You will also need to cut notches where the posts fit around the limestone railing cap. Check each post for plumb in both directions, and drive long lag

screws with washers to attach them to the railing's framing.

Cut and attach the beam pieces that run at right angles to and are parallel with the house. These fit into the notches you cut in the post tops. At the house, attach a ripped piece of cedar the same width as the notched post, and attach the beam pieces to each side of it. Cut the angled pieces, with 45-degree bevels at each end, and attach.

To come up with a rafter-end design that you like, work on a piece of cardboard or directly on a sample rafter end. Experiment using a compass or round objects, such as paint cans or jar lids, until you achieve a pleasing shape. Once you have cut the first rafter end, use it as a template for the others.

Install a ledger onto the house, its bottom level with the top of the beam. Use flashing or a hold-off method to ensure that water will not wick in and damage your house.

Lay out on top of the beams and on the ledger for evenly spaced rafters. Cut the rafters to length; the ones on the side get progressively shorter as they near the house. Attach to the ledger and the beam by drilling angled pilot holes and driving screws.

Lay out for evenly spaced top pieces, and attach by driving a screw into each joint.

THE LIMESTONE RAIL sits atop a short but beefed-up stud wall. Attach the stone to the top of the wall using an approved adhesive.

RESOURCE GUIDE

The following list of manufacturers and associations is meant to be a general guide to additional industry and product-related sources. It is not intended as a listing of products and manufacturers represented by the photographs in this book.

Advanced Concrete Enhancement
11070 Fleetwood St., Unit F
Sun Valley, CA 91352
818-504-0424
www.aceconrete.com
Manufactures decorative concrete kitchen sinks, countertops, surrounds, and flooring.

Alcoa Home Exteriors
201 Isabella St.
Pittsburgh, PA 15212-5858
800-962-6973
www.alcoa.com/alcoahomes
Manufactures aluminum and synthetic building materials, including deck products under the Oasis brand.

Alumatec Industries Inc.
529 Orange Ave.
Daytona, FL 32114
800-989-7245
www.alumatecindustries.com
Manufactures and installs a complete line of aluminum, stainless-steel, and brass railings.

Andersen Corporation
100 Fourth Ave. N.
Bayport, MN 55003-1096
800-426-4261
www.andersenwindows.com
Offers a full line of patio doors and windows.

APA – The Engineered Wood Association
7011 South 19th St.
Tacoma, WA 98466
253-565-6600
www.apawood.org
A nonprofit trade association that produces a variety of engineered-wood products.

AridDek
1604 Athens Hwy.
Gainesville, GA 30507
877-270-9387
www.ariddek.com
Manufactures aluminum decking and railings.

Arthur Lauer, Inc.
47 Steve's Ln.
Gardiner, NY 12525
845-255-2015
www.arthurlauer.com
Offers several lines of outdoor teak furniture, as well as rugs, pillows, and other products for outdoor living.

Atlantis Cabinetry
3304 Aerial Way Dr.
Roanoke, VA 24018
540-342-0363
www.atlantiscabinetry.com
Manufactures durable, polymer outdoor cabinetry in a variety of colors and designs.

AZEK Trimboards
801 Corey St.
Moosic, PA 18507
877-275-2935
www.azek.com
Makes synthetic trim products, including balustrades, moldings, and lattice skirting.

Baldwin Lawn Furniture
440 Middlefield St.
Middletown, CT 06457
800-344-5103
www.baldwinfurniture.com
Builds outdoor furniture, planters, and pergolas.

Blue Rhino Corporation
104 Cambridge Plaza Dr.
Winston-Salem, NC 27104
800-762-1142
www.uniflame.com
Offers a full line of grills, heaters, and other outdoor appliances, plus a propane tank exchange program.

CableRail/Feeney Architectural Products
2603 Union St.
Oakland, CA 94607
800-888-2418
www.cablerail.com
Manufactures a line of standard and custom cable stainless-steel cable assemblies.

Cal Spas
1462 East Ninth St.
Pomona, CA 91766
800-225-7727
www.calspas.com
Manufactures barbecue grills, islands, modular islands, fire pits, and fireplaces for the outdoors.

California Redwood Association
405 Enfrente Dr., Ste. 200
Novato, CA 94949-7206
888-225-7339
www.calredwood.org
Offers technical information about the use of redwood for decks and other structures.

Cascades
404 Marie-Victorin Blvd.
Kingsey Falls, QC, Canada J0A 1B0
819-363-5100
www.cascades.com
A packaging product leader that also makes decking from recycled plastic under the Perma-deck brand.

Cecco Trading, Inc.
600 East Vienna Ave.
Milwaukee, WI 53212
414-445-8989
www.ironwoods.com
Supplies the Iron Wood brand of Ipe hardwood lumber. Check the Web site to locate a lumber yard near you.

Classic Garden Design
1 Katydid Ln.
Weston, CT
203-226-2886
www.classicgardendesign.com
Designs and installs residential patios, perennial gardens, pergolas, walks, fences, and outdoor kitchens.

Consumer Product Safety Commission (CPSC)
4330 East West Hwy.
Bethesda, MD 20814
800-638-2772
www.cpsc.gov
Organization charged with protecting the public from unreasonable risks of serious injury or death from more than 15,000 types of consumer products.

Coolaroo
P.O. Box 951509
Lake Mary, FL 32795-1509
800-560-4667
www.coolaroo.com
Manufactures shade sails, umbrellas, and other shade devices that feature knitted outdoor fabric.

Correct Building Products
8 Morin St.
Biddeford, ME 04005
877-332-5877
www.correctdeck.com
Maker of CorrectDeck, a composite decking material.

Dacor
1440 Bridge Gate Dr.
Diamond Bar, CA 91765
800-793-0093
www.dacor.com
Designs and manufactures a full line of outdoor grills, built-in grills, grill carts, warming ovens, and side burners.

Deck Images
12590 127th St. S.
Hastings, MN 55033
877-446-7397
www.deckimages.com
Manufactures powder-coated aluminum and glass railing systems for residential and commercial markets.

Deckmaster
205 Mason Cir.
Concord, CA 94520
800-869-1375
www.deckmaster.com
Makes bracket-style hidden deck fasteners.

Deckorators
50 Crestwood Executive Center, Ste. 308
Crestwood, MO 63126
800-332-5724
www.deckorators.com
Manufactures a wide range of aluminum balustrades and glass railings in many colors and designs.

DekBrands
P.O. Box 14804
Minneapolis, MN 55414
800-664-2705
www.deckplans.com
Produces easy-to-do deck systems, including the award-winning Floating Foundation Deck System.

DESA
2701 Industrial Dr.
Bowling Green, KY 42101
866-672-6040
www.desatech.com
Maker of security lights with motion detectors and deck heaters, including umbrella stands with built-in heaters.

Dry-B-Lo
475 Tribble Gap Rd., Ste. 305
Cumming, GA 30040
800-437-9256
www.dry-b-lo.com
Manufactures aluminum deck drainage systems that keep the space below decks dry.

EB-TY Hidden Deck-Fastening Systems Blue Heron Enterprises, LLC
P.O. Box 5389
North Branch, NJ 08876
800-438-3289
www.ebty.com

Makes biscuit-style hidden deck fasteners.

Empyrean International, LLC

930 Main St.
Acton, MA 01720
800-727-3325
www.empyreanapf.com
Custom-designed homes that often feature decks. Brands include Deck House, Acorn, and The Dwell Homes by Empyrean.

EverGrain Composite Decking, a div. of TAMKO Building Products, Inc.

P.O. Box 1404
Joplin, MO 64802
800-253-1401
www.evergrain.com
Manufactures composite decking products with realistic, compression-molded graining patterns.

Forest Stewardship Council-U.S.

1155 30th St. NW, Ste. 300
Washington, D.C. 20007
202-342-0413
www.fscus.org
A nonprofit organization devoted to encouraging the responsible management of the world's forests.

Gaco Western

P.O. Box 88698
Seattle, WA 98138
866-422-6489
www.gaco.com
Manufactures a high-quality acrylic polymer waterproof surface protection for plywood or plank decks.

Gale Pacific

P.O. Box 951509

Lake Mary, FL 32795-1509
800-560-4667
www.coolaroo.com
Manufactures a wide range of outdoor fabrics with various degrees of UV protection.

Grace Construction Products

62 Whittemore Ave.
Cambridge, MA 02140
800-354-5414
www.graceconstruction.com
www.graceathome.com
Offers self-adhering flashing for decks.

Hadco Lighting, a div. of Genlyte Group Inc.

100 Craftway
Littlestown, PA 17340
800-331-4185
www.hadcolighting.com
Offers a large variety of outdoor lighting designed for decks, including post, step, path, and area lights.

Hearth & Home Technologies

20802 Kensington Blvd.
Lakeville, MN 55044
888-669-4328
www.hearthnhome.com
Offers a complete line of gas, electric, and wood-burning heating products.

Highpoint Deck Lighting

P.O. Box 428
Black Hawk, CO 80422
888-582-5850
www.hpdlighting.com
Produces a full line of outdoor lighting, including railing lights, recessed step lights, hanging lanterns, wall sconces, and barbecue cook lights.

Hooks and Lattice

5671 Palmer Way, Ste. K
Carlsbad, CA 92010
800-896-0978
www.hooksandlattice.com
Web site features all styles of window boxes designed for every application, including deck railings.

IntelliCool

1126 Commerce Dr.
Richardson, TX 75081
800-824-6567
www.intellicool.com
Manufactures outdoor climate- and environmental-control systems as well as a mosquito-repellant system.

Jacuzzi

14525 Monte Vista Ave.
Chino, CA 91710
866-234-7727
www.jacuzzi.com
Manufactures a full line of hot tubs and deck spas.

LockDry

FSI Home Products Division
2700 Alabama Hwy. 69 S.
Cullman, AL 35057
800-711-1785
www.lockdry.com
Patented aluminum deck and railing systems with built-in continuous gutters.

Marvin Windows and Doors

P.O. Box 100
Warroad, MN 56763
888-537-7828
www.marvin.com
Makers of windows and doors, including sliders and French doors.

NanaWall Systems, Inc.

707 Redwood Hwy.
Mill Valley, CA 94941
800-873-5673
www.nanawall.com
Manufactures folding wall systems of easy-to-open glass panels.

National Fenestration Rating Council (NFRC)

8484 Georgia Ave., Ste. 320
Silver Spring, MD 20910
301-589-1776
www.nfrc.org
A nonprofit organization that administers the only uniform, independent rating and labeling system for the energy performance of patio doors and other products.

Nautilus Cabinetry

4120 Enterprise Ave., Ste. 111
Naples, FL 34104
800-975-2805
www.nautiluscabinetry.com
Manufactures outdoor cabinetry constructed of marine polymer, teak, and cypress. Also offers a variety of outdoor refrigerators, grills, and range hoods.

Pella Corporation

102 Main St.
Pella, IA 50219
800-374-4758
www.pella.com
Produces energy-efficient patio doors and windows.

Procell Decking Systems

11746 Foley Beach Express
Foley, AL 36535
251-943-2916
www.procelldeck.com
Manufactures synthetic decking from PVC that's stain and scratch resistant.

Progress Lighting

P.O. Box 5704
Spartanburg, SC 29304-5704
864-599-6000
www.progresslighting.com
Makes wall lanterns that have motion detectors built into the mounting plate or the lantern itself, as well as deck and landscape lights.

Punch! Software, LLC

7900 NW 100th St., Ste. LL6
Kansas City, MO 64153
800-365-4832
www.punchsoftware.com
Software company specializing in home and landscaping design programs.

Royal Crown Limited

P.O. Box 360
Milford, IN 46542-0360
800-488-5245
www.royalcrownltd.com
Produces vinyl deck planks and railing products under the Triple Crown Fence, Brock Deck Systems, Brock Deck, and Deck Lok Systems brands.

Shade Sails LLC

7028 Greenleaf Ave., Ste. K
Whittier, CA 90602
562-945-9952
www.shadesails.com
Imports tensioned, UV-treated fabric canopies.

ShadeScapes USA

39300 Back River Rd.
Paonia, CO 81428
866-997-4233
www.shadescapesusa.com
Manufactures side- and center-post shade umbrellas.

Southern Pine Council

2900 Indiana Ave.
Kenner, LA 70065-4605
504-443-4464
www.southernpine.com
A trade association that offers information on deck building with treated lumber.

Starborn Industries, Inc.

27 Engelhard Ave.
Avenel, NJ 07001
800-596-7747
www.starbornindustries.com
Manufactures stainless-steel deck fastening systems, including Headcote and DeckFast brand screws.

Summer Classics

P.O. Box 390
7000 Hwy. 25
Montevallo, AL 35115
205-987-3100
www.summerclassics.com
Manufactures deck and garden furnishings in wrought aluminum, wrought iron and woven resin.

Summerwood Products

735 Progress Ave.
Toronto, ON, Canada M1H 2W7
866-519-4634
www.summerwood.com

Offers prefab customized kits for outdoor structures such as gazebos, pool cabanas, and spa enclosures.

Sundance Spas
14525 Monte Vista Ave.
Chino, CA 91710
800-883-7727
www.sundancespas.com
The largest manufacturer of acrylic spas.

Sustainable Forestry Initiative, a div. of American Forest & Paper Association
1111 Nineteenth St. NW, Ste. 800
Washington, D.C. 20036
www.aboutsfi.org
A comprehensive forestry management program developed by the American Forest & Paper Association.

TAMKO Building Products, Inc. EverGrain Composite Decking Elements Decking
220 West 4th St.
Joplin, MO 64801
800-641-4691
www.tamko.com
www.evergrain.com
www.elementsdecking.com
Manufactures composite decking products using compression molding for a real wood look. Visit the Web site for a photo gallery and distributors in your area.

Tiger Claw Inc.
400 Middle St., Ste. J
Bristol, CT 06010-8405
800-928-4437
www.deckfastener.com
Manufactures products for the construction industry, including hidden deck fasteners.

TimberTech
894 Prairie Ave.
Wilmington, OH 45177
800-307-7780
www.timbertech.com
Manufacturers composite decking and railing systems, fascia boards, and specialty trim.

Timber Treatment Technologies
8700 Trail Lake Dr., Ste. 101
Germantown, TN 38125
866-318-9432
www.timbersil.com
Developer of a new process for preserving wood. The formula, nontoxic and noncorrosive, is designed for both aboveground and in-ground applications.

Trex Company, Inc.
160 Exeter Dr.
Winchester, VA 22603
800-289-8739
www.trex.com
Specializes in composite decking materials.

Universal Forest Products, Inc.
2801 East Beltline Ave. NE
Grand Rapids, MI 49525
616-364-6161
www.ufpi.com
Manufactures and distributes wood and wood-alternative products for decking and railing systems. Also manufactures Veranda brand products.

Western Red Cedar Lumber Association (WRCLA)
1501-700 W. Pender St.
Pender Place 1, Business Building
Vancouver, BC, Canada V6C 1G8
866-778-9096
www.realcedar.org

www.wrcla.org
www.cedar-deck.org
A nonprofit trade association representing quality producers of western red cedar in the U.S. and Canada. Its Web site explains how to select appropriate grades.

Weyerhaeuser Co.
P.O. Box 1237
Springdale, AR 72765
800-951-5117
www.choicedek.com
Offers ChoiceDek brand decking manufactured from a blend of low- and high-density polyethylene plastic and wood fibers. Also distributes CedarOne cedar decking.

Wolman Wood Care Products, a div. of Zinsser Co., Inc.
173 Belmont Dr.
Somerset, NJ 08875
800-556-7737
www.wolman.com
Makes products used to restore, beautify, and protect decks and other exterior wood structures.

GLOSSARY

Actual dimensions The exact measurements of a piece of lumber after it has been cut, surfaced, and dried. For example, a 2×4's actual dimensions are 1½ × 3½ inches.

Balusters The numerous vertical pieces, often made of 2×2s or 1×4s, that fill in spaces between rails and provide a fence-like structure.

Band joist Any joist that defines the perimeter of a deck, including the header joist and end, or outside, joists. Also called rim joist.

Beam A large framing member, usually four-by material or doubled-up two-bys, which is attached horizontally to the posts and used to support joists.

Blocking Usually solid pieces of lumber the same dimensions as the joists, which are cut to fit snugly between the joists to prevent excessive warping. Also called bridging or bracing.

Building codes Municipal rules regulating safe building practices and procedures. Generally, the codes encompass structural, electrical, plumbing, and mechanical remodeling and new construction. Confirmation of conformity to local codes by inspection may be required.

Building permit A license that authorizes permission to do work on your home. Minor repairs and remodeling work usually do not call for a permit, but if the job consists of extending the water supply and drain, waste, vent system; adding an electrical circuit; or making structural changes to a building, a building permit may be necessary.

Cantilever Construction that extends beyond its vertical support.

Curing The slow chemical action that hardens concrete.

Decking Boards nailed to joists to form the deck surface.

Elevation Architectural drawing of a structure seen from the side, rear, or front view.

Fascia board Facing that covers the exposed ends and sides of decking to provide a finished appearance.

Footing The concrete base that supports posts or steps.

Frost line The maximum depth to which soil freezes. The local building department can provide information on the frost line depth in your area.

Grade The ground level. On-grade means at or on the natural ground level.

Header joist Band joist attached and running at a right angle to common joists, enabling them to maintain correct spacing and stiffening their ends.

Joist Structural member, usually two-by lumber, commonly placed perpendicularly across beams to support deck boards.

Joist hanger Metal connector used to join a joist and beam so that the tops are in the same plane.

Knot The high-density root of a limb that is very dense but is not connected to the surrounding wood.

Lag screw Large wood screw (usually ¼ inch or more in diameter) with a bolt-like hex head usually used to attached ledgers to house framing. Often incorrectly called lag bolt.

Lattice A cross-pattern structure that is made of wood, metal, or plastic.

Ledger Horizontal board attached to the side of a house or wall to support a deck or an overhead cover.

Nominal dimensions The identifying dimensions of a piece of lumber (e.g. 2×4) which are larger than the actual dimensions (1½ × 3½).

Penny (abbreviated "d") Unit of measurement for nail length; e.g., a 10d nail is 3 inches long.

Permanent structure Any structure that is anchored to the ground or a house.

Plan drawing A drawing which gives an overhead view of the deck showing where all footings and lumber pieces go.

Plumb Vertically straight, in relation to a horizontally level surface.

Plunge cut A cut that can't begin from the outside of the board and must be made from the middle.

Post A vertical member, usually 4×4 or 6×6, that supports either the deck or railing.

Post anchor A metal fastener designed to keep the post from wandering and also to inhibit rot by holding the post a bit above the concrete.

Posthole digger A clamshell-type tool used to dig holes for posts.

Power auger A tool that is powered by a gasoline engine and used for drilling into the ground. Often used in larger projects to dig postholes.

Pressure-treated lumber Wood that has had preservatives forced into it under

pressure to make it repel rot and insects.

On center A point of reference for measuring. For example, "16 inches on center" means 16 inches from the center of one framing member to the center of the next.

Rabbet A ledge cut along one edge of a workpiece.

Rail A horizontal member that is placed between posts and used for support or as a barrier.

Railing Assembly made from balusters attached to rails and installed between posts as a safety barrier at the edge of a deck.

Railing cap A horizontal piece of lumber laid flat on top of the post and top rail, covering the end grain of the post and providing a flat surface wide enough to set objects on.

Recommended span The distance a piece of lumber can safely traverse without being supported underneath.

Redwood A straight-grain, weather-resistant wood used for outdoor building.

Rim joist *See* Band joist.

Rip cut A cut made with the grain on a piece of wood.

Riser Vertical boards placed between stringers on stairs to support stair treads. They are optional on exterior stairs.

Site plan A drawing which maps out your house and yard. Also called a base plan.

Skewing Driving two nails at opposing angles. This technique creates a sounder connection by "hooking" the boards together as well as by reducing the possibility of splitting.

Skirt Solid band of horizontal wood members (fascia) installed around the deck perimeter to conceal exposed ends of joists and deck boards.

Stringer On stairs, the diagonal boards that support the treads and risers; also called a stair horse.

Tack-nail To nail one structural member to another temporarily with a minimal amount of nails.

Toenail Joining two boards together by nailing at an angle through the end, or toe, on one board and into the face of another.

Tread On stairs, the horizontal boards supported by the stringers.

INDEX

PHOTO CREDITS

All photos by Steve Cory unless otherwise noted.

page 1: Clemens Jellema **page 6:** *upper middle* Kim Katwijk bottom Clemens Jellema **page 7:** *bottom* Dave Toht **page 8:** Clemens Jellema **pages 12–14:** Dave Toht, builder: Kim Katwijk **page 15:** *top* courtesy of Southern Forest Products Association **page 16:** courtesy of California Redwood Association **page 17:** *top left* Dave Toht builder: Kim Katwijk; *top right* courtesy of California Redwood Association; *bottom* courtesy of Tamko/EverGrain **page 18:** *top left* DeckSouth; *top right* courtesy of California Redwood Association; *bottom* courtesy of Trex **pages 20–21:** *left* Kim Katwijk; *top right* courtesy of California Redwood Association; *bottom right* courtesy of Elyria Fence Inc. **page 22:** *bottom left & right* courtesy of Southern Forest Products Association **page 24:** *top* courtesy of Tamko/EverGrain **page 26:** *top* Kim Katwijk; *bottom* courtesy of Trex Company, Inc. **page 27:** courtesy of Western Red Cedar Lumber Association **page 28:** *top* courtesy of Tamko/EverGrain; *bottom left* courtesy of Heat & Glo **page 29:** DeckSouth **page 30:** Kim Katwijk **page 31:** *bottom* courtesy of Hadco Lighting **page 33:** *bottom* courtesy of Tamko/EverGrain **pages 38–39:** *left* courtesy of Trex Company, Inc. **page 41:** *top* Clemens Jellema **page 42:** *top* Dave Toht **page 45:** DeckSouth **page 47:** *bottom* DeckSouth **page 49:** *all* DeckSouth **page 51:** *top left* DeckSouth **page 88:** *top right* Clemens Jellema **pages 89–90:** *all* Clemens Jellema **page 91:** *top* Clemens Jellema **page 92:** Clemens Jellema **page 94:** *top* Clemens Jellema **page 95:** *bottom* Clemens Jellema **pages 96–97:** Clemens Jellema **page 98:** *top* Clemens Jellema **page 100:** *top* Clemens Jellema **page 101:** *all* Clemens Jellema **page 102:** *bottom* Clemens Jellema **page 103:** *top right, center & bottom* Clemens Jellema **page 104:** Clemens Jellema **page 105:** *bottom* Clemens Jellema **page 108:** *all* Clemens Jellema **page 111:** Clemens Jellema **page 124:** Clemens Jellema **page 125:** *bottom* Clemens Jellema **pages 130–131:** *all* Clemens Jellema **page 134:** *left* Dave Toht; *top & bottom* Kim Katwijk **page 135:** Dave Toht **page 136:** *top* Dave Toht; *bottom* Kim Katwijk **page 137:** *bottom* Dave Toht **page 138:** *right* Kim Katwijk; *left* Dave Toht **page 139:** Dave Toht **pages 140–141:** *all* Kim Katwijk **page 143:** *all* Dave Toht **page 145:** *top & bottom left* Dave Toht; *bottom right* Kim Katwijk **page 146:** *top & bottom* Dave Toht **page 147:** Dave Toht **pages 151–152:** *all* Kim Katwijk **page 159:** *all* Kim Katwijk **pages 160–161:** all Dave Toht **page 164:** all Dave Toht **pages 169-170:** all Kim Katwijk **page 171:** *top and bottom* Kim Katwijk; *right* Dave Toht **pages 172–173:** *all* Dave Toht **pages 175–180:** *all* Kim Katwijk **page 181:** *all* Kim Katwijk; *bottom left* Dave Toht **page 228:** Dave Toht **page 231:** Dave Toht **page 233:** Clemens Jellema

Metric Equivalents

Length

1 inch	25.4 mm
1 foot	0.3048 m
1 yard	0.9144 m
1 mile	1.61 km

Area

1 square inch	645 mm^2
1 square foot	0.0929 m^2
1 square yard	0.8361 m^2
1 acre	4046.86 m^2
1 square mile	2.59 km^2

Volume

1 cubic inch	16.3870 cm^3
1 cubic foot	0.03 m^3
1 cubic yard	0.77 m^3

Common Lumber Equivalents

Sizes: Metric cross sections are so close to their U.S. sizes, as noted below, that for most purposes they may be considered equivalents.

Dimensional lumber	1 × 2	19 × 38 mm
	1 × 4	19 × 89 mm
	2 × 2	38 × 38 mm
	2 × 4	38 × 89 mm
	2 × 6	38 × 140 mm
	2 × 8	38 × 184 mm
	2 × 10	38 × 235 mm
	2 × 12	38 × 286 mm
Sheet sizes	4 × 8 ft.	1200 × 2400 mm
	4 × 10 ft.	1200 × 3000 mm
Sheet thicknesses	¼ in.	6 mm
	⅜ in.	9 mm
	½ in.	12 mm
	¾ in.	19 mm
Stud/joist spacing	16 in. o.c.	400 mm o.c.
	24 in. o.c.	600 mm o.c.

Capacity

1 fluid ounce	29.57 mL
1 pint	473.18 mL
1 quart	1.14 L
1 gallon	3.79 L

Weight

1 ounce	28.35g
1 pound	0.45kg

Temperature

Fahrenheit = Celsius × 1.8 + 32

Celsius = Fahrenheit − 32 × 5⁄9

Nail Size & Length

Penny Size	Nail Length
2d	1"
3d	1¼"
4d	1½"
5d	1¾"
6d	2"
7d	2¼"
8d	2½"
9d	2¾"
10d	3"
12d	3¼"
16d	3½"

Have a home improvement, decorating, or gardening project? Look for these and other fine Creative Homeowner books wherever books are sold.

Ultimate Guide to Decks
Step-by-step deck building for the novice.
Over 750 photos and illustrations.
288 pp.; 8^1/$_2$" × 10^7/$_8$"
BOOK#: 277168

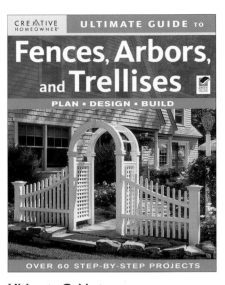

**Ultimate Guide to
Fences, Arbors and Trellises**
Step-by-step guide to building fences, arbors, and trellises. Over 825 color photos and illustrations. 288 pp.; 8^1/$_2$" × 10^7/$_8$"
BOOK #: 277990

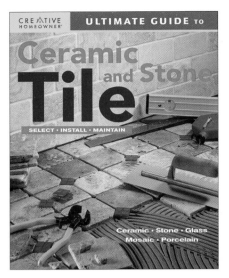

**Ultimate Guide to
Ceramic Tile and Stone**
Complete DIY tile instruction. Over 550 color photos and illustrations.
224 pp.; 8^1/$_2$" × 10^7/$_8$"
BOOK #: 277532

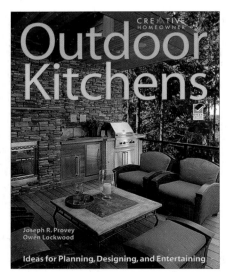

Outdoor Kitchens
Showcases fully equipped year-round designs for every budget and any part of the country. Over 320 photographs.
224 pp; 8^1/$_2$" × 10^7/$_8$"
BOOK #: 277571

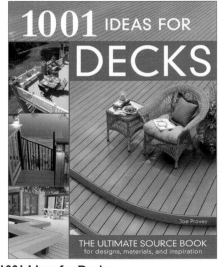

1001 Ideas for Decks
Covers design solutions, building techniques, and the latest information on deck materials. Over 450 photographs.
288 pp.; 8^1/$_2$" × 10^7/$_8$"
BOOK #: 277194

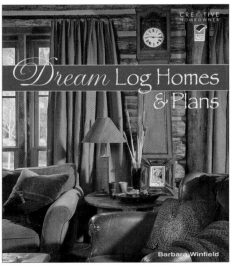

Dream Log Homes & Plans
Great ideas for designing, buying, building and furnishing an ideal log home.
240 pp.; 9^1/$_4$" × 10^7/$_8$"
BOOK #276158

For more information and to order direct, visit our Web site at **www.creativehomeowner.com**